THE ARAB
AND THE AFRICAN

EXPERIENCES IN EASTERN EQUATORIAL AFRICA
DURING A RESIDENCE OF THREE YEARS

BY

S. TRISTRAM PRUEN, M.D.
Fellow of the Royal Geographical Society

WITH ILLUSTRATIONS

DARF PUBLISHERS LIMITED
LONDON
1986

FIRST PUBLISHED 1891
NEW IMPRESSION 1986

ISBN 978 1 850 77136 4

TO

COLONEL SIR CHARLES EUAN-SMITH

K.C.B., C.S.I.,

LATE HER MAJESTY'S AGENT AND CONSUL-GENERAL AT ZANZIBAR,
NOW HER MAJESTY'S MINISTER AT THE COURT OF MOROCCO,

WHO HAS WORKED SO EARNESTLY FOR THE ABOLITION OF
SLAVERY; AND WHO, BY HIS JUDGMENT, TACT,
AND UNSELFISH DEVOTION TO DUTY,
HAS AT LAST PLACED FREEDOM WITHIN THE REACH OF
MILLIONS OF HIS FELLOW CREATURES ON THE
DARK CONTINENT OF AFRICA,

THIS BOOK IS DEDICATED,

WITH THE AUTHOR'S MOST SINCERE RESPECT AND
ADMIRATION.

PREFACE

THE author has endeavoured in this book to describe in detail the daily life of the natives of Central Africa who live in and around the districts which have so recently been brought under British influence. He has also discussed the results of endeavouring to bring the untutored native, all unprepared, suddenly under the influence of laws and customs which have been gradually developed elsewhere through thirty generations of progressive civilization. He believes that the facts thus brought forward will be of interest to all who thoughtfully consider the ever-widening boundaries, and ever-increasing responsibilities of the great Empire to which they belong.

He also hopes that what he has written will supply two distinct wants; the want felt by the Philanthropist at home, who wishes to study the Slave

Trade in all its bearings, and that felt by the Missionary or Trader who, about to proceed to East Equatorial Africa, desires to know what he is likely to meet with there, and what preparations he should make before going.

He has limited himself, as far as possible, to describing what he has actually seen and heard. He hopes that his book may throw some new light upon the Slave Trade, and the daily life of the African, as it is written by one who has lived amongst the people as their friend and equal, and who has thus been permitted to see and hear things hidden from the passing traveller, and even from the resident who rules over rather than lives amongst the people with whom he is brought into daily contact. He has been much encouraged in this hope by a letter from Sir C. B. Euan-Smith, who, in kindly accepting the dedication of the book, expressed his opinion that it would supply a distinct want.

Uganda has been left entirely out of account in the descriptions, partly because the Waganda differ in so many points from other East African races, and partly because they have been so fully described by Mr. Ashe, in his interesting book, 'Two Kings of Uganda.'

The chapter on Diseases is necessarily incomplete

Preface

in a book intended for general circulation; but the author hopes shortly to publish, for the use of non-medical travellers, a separate pamphlet containing more full information on this point, together with hints on the diagnosis and treatment of the more common diseases met with in East Africa.

Lastly, the author wishes to acknowledge the debt of gratitude he owes to many kind friends who have helped him much in getting the book into shape. Especially is he indebted to his cousin, Mr. G. G. Pruen, of Cheltenham College, whose advice on many points has been invaluable; to the lady who took much pains in arranging the music in Chapter III.; to that other lady who, with very poor materials as copies, succeeded in producing illustrations both accurate and artistic; and to Mr. Seeley, for whose kind encouragement and assistance he feels truly grateful.

CHELTENHAM, 1891.

CONTENTS

CHAPTER	PAGE
I. THE LAND	1
II. THE VEGETATION AND ANIMALS	18
III. THE PEOPLE	62
IV. THE DAILY LIFE OF THE PEOPLE	107
V. THE CLIMATE AND DISEASES	142
VI. THE TRAVELLER	152
VII. A DAY'S MARCH	187
VIII. THE SLAVE-TRADE	208
IX. THE SLAVE	233
X. THE ARAB	249
XI. THE MISSIONARY	263
XII. THE MISSIONARY (*continued*)	289

LIST OF ILLUSTRATIONS

	PAGE
PORTRAIT OF SIR C. B. EUAN-SMITH, K.C.B.	*Frontispiece*
GERMAN AND BRITISH COASTS	4
VILLAGE IN USAGARA	8
MAP OF ELEVATIONS	16
BAOBOB-TREE	19
GUN-TRAP	34
ANTELOPE HUNTED BY DOGS	38
HORNBILL	47
THE MANTIS	55
AFRICAN SMITHY	78
HOE, AXE, BILLHOOK, ETC.	79
HOOKAH	85
SPEARS AND KNOBKERRIES	89
OBTAINING SAP FROM THE COCOANUT-TREE	105
BANJO	106
TEMBÉS IN UGOGO	118
THE ESPLANADE, ZANZIBAR	162
PAYING POSHO	172
ARAB KILLING A WORN-OUT SLAVE	220
MAP OF THE SLAVE-TRADE	226
HOUSES FOR EUROPEANS	279
HUTS FOR SICK NATIVES	307

The Arab and the African

CHAPTER I

THE LAND

THE tropical Africa of our childhood, with its unknown interior and imaginary sandy wastes stretching from sea to sea, is a thing of the past, and in its place we have a country containing great lakes and magnificent rivers; whilst the maps which depict it are traversed by scores of lines, the routes of the soldier, the missionary and the explorer. Yet, notwithstanding all these advances, but few of us realize the home-life of the people, or rather peoples, of Central Africa, or understand the wide-reaching inclusive nature of the political system known as slavery, and the insurmountable barrier which it presents to the missionary and the trader.

An Englishman cannot grasp what is included under that one term 'slavery' unless he first understands the people, and to understand them he needs to know the country. Slavery is no such simple system as we of the West are apt to understand by the term. It is not solely a question of the brutal Arab, with his semi-civilization, lording it over and ill-treating the innocent and ingenuous occupier of the soil. The Arab has right, as well as wrong, on his side. The system of slavery has its advantages few and far between, as well as its disadvantages many and frequent, some glaring and evident, others unknown and unsuspected. As a whole, the system is detestable—the slave-dealer is frequently brutal; the slave often ill-treated. Yet, if we examine the matter fairly, we shall see that the dealer has something to say on his own behalf—has some points in his favour which we have no right to overlook, however much we may rightly abhor and condemn the system; and that the slave is not always to be pitied, and must sometimes be condemned—and none the less condemned, because on many points he ought to be sympathised with and helped, and, above all things, freed. It would be a glorious deed to abolish African slavery in the century which gave birth to Livingstone, and saw him spend his life in the noble endeavour to heal the open sore of the world; but a deed which we shall never hasten by shutting our eyes to the defects of the slave or the good points of the Arab. The Eastern mind resents injustice fiercely; and in our condemnation of the slave-trade, we of the West are in danger of being unjust to the Arabs through insufficient knowledge of the conditions of life that prevail in Central Africa. It may help us perhaps to judge the Arab more justly, and with more of sorrow than anger, if we recollect that England has been one of the greatest of slave-trading nations; and that even in the present century English enterprise and English capital have largely contributed to the maintenance of this traffic.

Tropical Africa is the great cradle of the slave-trade, and for a century it has been very largely at the mercy of the Arab; but now the European has begun to step in, and its eastern half has become the sphere of operation of three great companies — two British companies to the north and to the south, with a German one between them. It is to this eastern half that our attention is to be directed.

As the traveller steams northward along the eastern coast from the southern limit of the dominions of the Sultan of Zanzibar, he notices the low-lying region that skirts the Indian Ocean; whilst lying behind, more or less dim in the perpetual African haze, he sees a range of hills, replaced in some parts by gently-rising ground. This marshy coast-line, malarious and deadly, which at Bagamoyo is about ten miles wide, becomes narrowed at Saadani, opposite the town of Zanzibar, to four miles, and finally terminates north of this before reaching Pangani, from which point northwards the coast rises abruptly in coral limestone rocks to a height of fifty feet or more. Thus the British company, whose territory does not reach so far south as Pangani, has no marshy coast-line, no unhealthy ports.

Behind the marsh to the south, and behind the shore to the north, the land rises by a gradual slope of eighty miles to a height of about fifteen hundred feet, from which, in the German region, stretches the first or coast plateau for eighty miles inland, in many parts broken up by spurs of the adjacent mountain-range, but in others extending for many days' march together in an almost unbroken level, with scenery not unlike that of the fen-country at home. It is a continuous swamp all through the rainy season, a monotonous plain in the dry one, traversed by a few large streams, and consequently

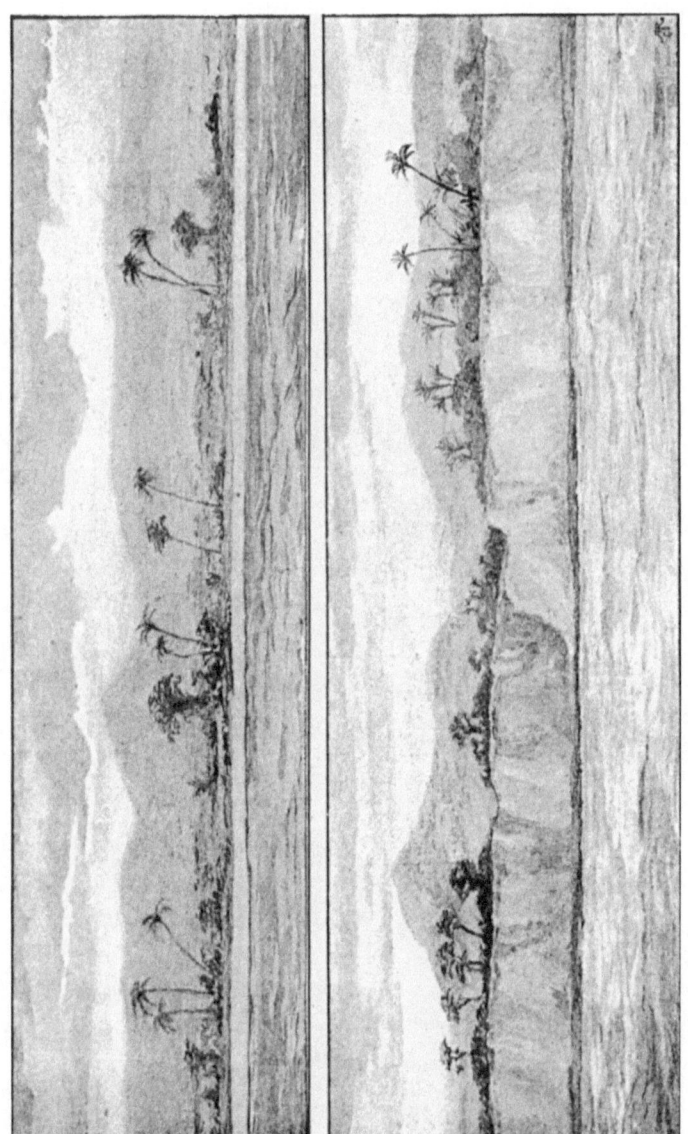

GERMAN AND BRITISH COASTS.

better covered with vegetation than most parts. Having crossed this plain, the traveller is confronted by precipitous rocks, and a march or climb of eighty miles over rugged passes from four to five thousand feet above the sea-level, and along the sides of steep inclines, takes him over a narrowed portion of the great mountain-range which stretches in an almost unbroken chain from the Cape of Good Hope to Abyssinia. Once across this range, he is landed on the second or great plateau of Central Africa, which stretches across the Continent at an elevation of three to four thousand feet. A very striking feature is this mountain-chain, sharply cutting off the lower coast plateau and rising ground from the great central plain of the Continent, and leaving each flank with features peculiar to itself.

Like the low-lying coast-region, the first or narrow plateau, which is eighty miles wide in the German region, gradually narrows to unimportant dimensions as it passes northwards into the British district, being encroached upon by the great mountain-chain, which here widens its flanks, preparatory to rising in terrace after terrace to the clouds, and then piercing through and towering far above them in the giant hills of Kenia and Kilimanjaro.

Hitherto Bagamoyo and Saadani have been the

ports from which most of the traffic has been carried on with the interior, along the great slave-routes stretching from these points to the ports on Tanganyika and Victoria Nyanza. 'Roads' they are called, but the term 'paths' would more correctly convey their condition to the Western mind; for they are only narrow tracks from nine to fifteen inches wide, bared of vegetation by the frequent tramping of naked feet, but as uneven as when originally made.

As the traveller marches from Saadani westwards, he leaves at once behind him the two-storied houses of the coast and the tropical-looking cocoanut-palms; and soon there is little to remind him that he has left his Western home so far away. He walks through continual woodland, not unlike the outskirts of Epping Forest in the late autumn, except for an occasional cactus-like euphorbia; a baobob, looking for all the world like a tree put in the wrong way up; or a still more occasional wild banana or fan-palm. Here and there at long intervals he comes upon some evidently better-watered spot than usual—perhaps upon some long low valley amongst the hills, where typical tropical trees are thicker and more frequent, with an abundance of rank grass and undergrowth amongst

them, giving the whole scene the appearance of one
of our English country parks run wild.

On the first plateau, as we have noticed, there are
a few large rocky streams, along whose banks rise
fine and shady trees ; but elsewhere all up the
hill and mountain sides, and in unending succession
along the plains, come forest after forest of low scrub
or dwarfed thorn-trees, whose spiny leaves and
scanty foliage give little shelter from the tropical
sun ; mile after mile of shadeless forest, a monotonous sameness broken only by the occasional
euphorbia or baobob; with a few scanty flowers and
still fewer fruits, bitter and acid, or tasteless. At
intervals of about ten miles from each other, and
therefore, for porters with loads, at about a day's
march distant, come villages, all constructed much
in the same way. A double fence surrounds the
village, and between the two fences, which are some
ten yards apart, are tall shrubs and small trees.
There are one or two entrances through the
shrubbery, guarded at either end by narrow doorways, which can be easily blocked. Inside are the
houses, low, circular huts of wickerwork and mud,
with thatched roofs ; seldom over twenty houses in a
village, sometimes not a dozen. Near the villages the
ground is mostly cultivated, millet-seed, Indian corn,

sweet potatoes, beans, pumpkins, and tobacco forming the staple products; cassava, sugar-cane, rice, bananas, papaye, guavas, limes, and ground-nuts the exceptional ones. The uncultivated ground is used for grazing cattle, goats, a few sheep, and a very occasional donkey, besides which innumerable fowls pick up a scanty living. On the coast-plateau, however, there are hardly any cattle, as the tsetse fly holds almost undisputed sway over the whole of this belt of land. The tsetse is an insect in shape and size like an ordinary house-fly, and in colour not unlike the bee, with three or four dull-yellow bars across the back of the abdomen. This fly attacks man and animal indiscriminately, but the bite is dangerous only to some of the latter. We were frequently badly bitten by this little pest, which is very rapid in its movements, and very persistent in returning to the victim it has commenced to attack. It is only in the cool of the early morning, or in the late evening, before it has retired to its well-earned rest, that the lower temperature seems to partially benumb it, and render it an easy prey to the wrath of its victim. When it alights, the tsetse inserts its long proboscis into the skin of its victim, a somewhat painful proceeding, which, however, has no apparent effect beyond the transient pain of the insertion, except in

VILLAGE IN USAGARA.

the case of horses, cattle, and dogs, and occasionally donkeys. When one of these animals has been bitten, it does not suffer at first; and if it be in good health, it may not show any symptoms for a week or ten days, but at the end of this time it begins to refuse its food, and to fail in health. The first symptoms are variable, but usually flaccidity of muscles, and, consequently, a staggering walk are amongst the earliest. Next blindness ensues from commencing opacity in the internal media of the eye, the whole eye presenting a semi-transparent greenish appearance. If the animal lives long enough, the fact that it is suffering from true blood-poisoning will be made evident by the appearance of abscesses in many of its joints, which enlarge quickly, but which do not appear to cause it much pain.

The streams of this plateau are not many in number, and are all fordable, most of them being only one or two feet deep. The fish in them are said to be few and small, but I have never seen a specimen, so cannot vouch for the truth of this statement. I do not think fishing can be much practised, as, though I took a great many fishhooks up country with me for barter, I never managed to dispose of one. Apparently, the crocodile and the hippopotamus are the only inhabitants of these waters. The former do not seem dangerous to people, to adults, at least, but are so to goats and dogs. The European must look sharply after his dogs, or they may be snapped up, as they are not so wary as the native dog, who, when he goes to drink, first looks carefully this way and that before venturing to slake his thirst. The European dog has no such instinct, but boldly plunges in; he likes not only to drink, but to lie down in the shallow waters, and cool his burning skin, and unfortunately the crocodile likes to do the same. Along these same rivers grow ferns which cannot flourish in the drier districts. Up amongst the hill-streams different varieties of maiden-hair are common; here, too, are orchids, which, abounding in East Africa, naturally grow more plentifully on the well-foliaged trees, which are only to be found along the river sides.

In the wet season the ground is swampy for miles along the plateau, but during the dry season many of the smaller streams are empty, and water can only be obtained by digging in their beds wells of a depth which it is necessary gradually to increase as the dry months pass by. At one place where we camped towards the end of the dry season, the natives had to dig fifteen feet below the river bed before they struck water. Again, in the wet season, such is the abundance of water under the surface everywhere that it sends up a mist in the mornings unknown in the drier regions of the central plateau. I remember on one occasion some Wagogo from the dry and almost waterless region of Ugogo, who were coming down to the coast for the first time, were amazed beyond measure to see the sun look a reddish-yellow through the early morning mist, a condition absolutely unknown to them in the whole of their experience. No one could persuade them that it was not the moon, and it was not until it rose far above the horizon, and the mists began to disappear, that they were convinced that we had not been endeavouring to impose upon them.

The smell from these swampy districts is at times quite sickening; but for pungency of odour and really disgusting fœtor, there is nothing to equal that resulting from the first rains, which at the end of a dry season begin to soak into, and thereby decompose, the accumulated surface refuse of months.

Wild animals are plentiful all along this plateau, but they are much more plentiful and varied in the hills, and will be better considered in the description of those regions.

After eighty miles of the dead level we have been describing, the traveller reaches the commencement of the great mountain range, and now for another eighty miles his way lies over hill after hill, bare rugged paths across the sharp granite and quartz rocks, and still through unending forest. Here he is amongst the Wasagara, and gradually the style of huts begins to change. At first he sees the usual villages, but with only a single surrounding fence, perched on the top of ridges or conical eminences or other commanding situations for safety; but these gradually give place to the well-known buildings called 'tembés,' the regulation house or hut of Central Africa. These tembés are all alike, except in size. Each consists of a kind of covered passage built round a square courtyard. The passages are built of stout, upright poles, less than six feet high, with strong wickerwork in between, the interstices being filled in with mud. The doors are also constructed of stout wickerwork, and slide clumsily from side to side. The upright poles are so short that an ordinary-sized man cannot stand upright inside. I think the natives do not stay indoors much; indeed, there is not much to tempt them to do so, the huts being very stuffy in dry weather, while in wet weather they let in the rain. Each passage is sub-divided by incomplete partitions of strong wickerwork, and several families live in one tembé, having each of them two or three divisions, as not only they, but all their herds come inside at night for protection from the wild animals.

Once over this range the traveller finds himself on the grand plateau, and begins to realize that he is truly in Central Africa, cut off from even the semi-civilization of Zanzibar, and in an altogether new world.

By far the most important village along the western flank of the range is Mpwapwa, the great junction for the trade routes, or in other words for the slave routes, of Eastern Equatorial Africa. Many routes converge here from the Victoria Nyanza and Tanganyika, and diverge again as they pass eastward to the different ports on the East African Coast. Stanley, in his 'Dark Continent,' describes Mpwapwa as lying in 'a deep indentation in the great mountain chain that extends from Abyssinia, or even Suez, down to the Cape of Good Hope.' This indentation is about twenty miles deep, and does not by any means cut through the ridge; the hill of Mpwapwa standing boldly up as the Eastern rampart against the encroaching plain. This great undulating plain, the central plateau of which we have been speaking, formed locally of red sands and clay, reaches in one unbroken level to the shores of Tanganyika and the Victoria Nyanza; whilst the gentle declivities down the valleys of the Nile and Congo give it an exit to the Mediterranean and Atlantic. Hence it is that swallows which leave our coasts in October can pass up the Nile and across the great plain to Mpwapwa and other villages at the base of the mountain chain, where they stay until February. Numbers of them reach this western flank, but none ever pass further east. I have lived amongst the hills only four miles east of Mpwapwa for an entire winter without ever seeing a single swallow there, although each time that I crossed the hill to Mpwapwa, I saw them in numbers.

As a rule the same variety of bird is common to the greater part of the central plateau; for instance the same varieties occur at Mpwapwa and on the shores of Tanganyika and the Victoria Nyanza; whilst varieties which abound in Zanzibar and on the East coast are much less common on the plateau. There are, however, exceptions to this rule, as many birds do not seem to find the hills, with their many passes at an elevation of only five thousand feet, any real barrier. This mountain chain, as has been mentioned before, abounds in game of all kinds, the descriptions of which will come more naturally in the Chapter on Animals.

I know no one familiar with the western flank of

The German Territory

the chain higher up in the German and English districts, but I expect the description of the country round about Mpwapwa answers fairly well for the flank further north.

The difference between the British and German districts appears to be caused by the varying width of the mountain chain. The coast swamp which is such a feature in the German is wanting in the British territory. The marshy coast plateau, which is something under one hundred miles wide in the German, almost disappears in the English territory, encroached upon, as we have seen, by the widening eastern flanks of Kilimanjaro and Kenia. The high tableland of the great central plateau is also pushed further westward towards the north, encroached upon in the same way by the western flanks of these great mountains. With the presence of the marshy plateau, the Germans have also a monopoly of the tsetse fly, which is absent, I believe in the British territory, or at the worst, exists only in a narrow belt, easily passable in one night, and is therefore avoidable by caravans passing through.

The annexed map represents the difference between the two districts; but very diagrammatically. From the regions which I have visited myself in the southern German territory, and from the descriptions

16   *The Land*

given me by friends who have travelled in the northern portions of the German and in the English territories, it seems evident that the features of the country are much the same in any latitude where

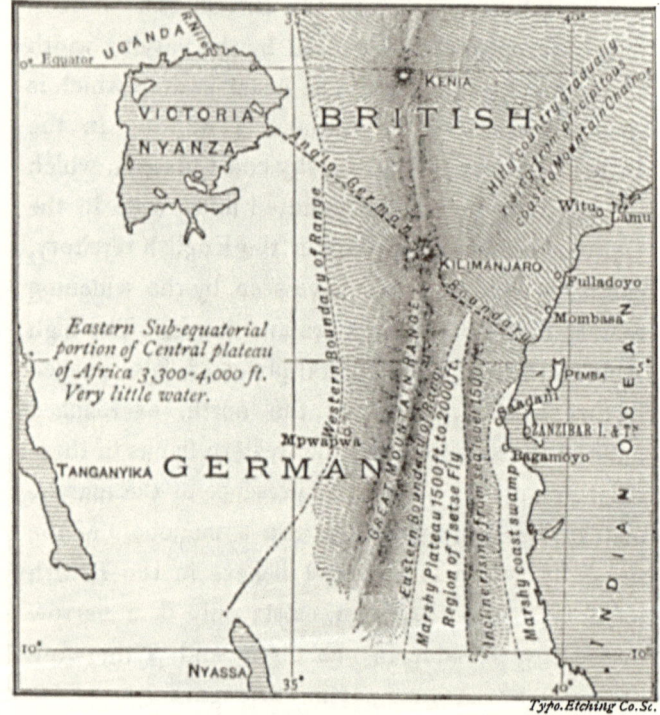

the same elevation is reached. Thus the features of the incline are the same whether north or south, and so are the features of the central plateau. But although it is east and west not north and south that really determines the different features, yet the narrowing of some districts from east to west in different latitudes completely alters the conditions existing north and south, when Eastern Equatorial Africa is considered as a whole. The German physical districts are all, with the exception of the coast marsh, represented in the English territory, and *vice versâ;* but the districts which are wide in one are narrow in the other, hence the marked difference north and south, and hence also, the marked superiority of the British over the German territory.

The mountain chain at the latitude of Mpwapwa, which abounds in granite, gneiss, schists and serpentine, is also rich in metals, amongst which I believe I have seen gold in the quartz not far from Mpwapwa. After finding much pyrites, the German in command at Mpwapwa, Herr Krieger (who was killed soon afterwards by the Arabs at Kilwa, to which port he had been sent to take charge of it), showed me a specimen of what I thought at the time was native gold, and examination of museum specimens since my return to England has convinced me that it was really so. The formation being the same, there is, I suppose, a probability of gold being discovered in the same chain further north in British territory.

CHAPTER II

THE VEGETATION AND ANIMALS

AFTER leaving the coast, the first feature in the landscape that strikes the European is, as mentioned in the last chapter, the similarity of the vegetation to that met with at home, especially in districts where conifers predominate. At the coast itself, and on the adjacent islands, the palms, baobobs, mangoes, oranges, limes, cloves, bananas, pine-apples, and jack-fruit give the landscape a truly tropical appearance, quite unlike that with which the dweller in temperate climes is familiar; but elsewhere all this changes, and there are few edible fruits, the natives of the interior paying little or no attention to their culture. In a very few villages the banana, the papaye, and the guava are cultivated; and in one or two isolated spots where the Arab or European has settled, he has brought seeds or cuttings, and planted a few other fruit-trees. Tamarinds, wild grapes, and species of wild cherry and wild mango are not uncommon; but they are not very acceptable to the European palate, nor do they appear to be prized even by the native. This absence of fruit of any kind is very trying to the

BAOBOB TREE

traveller in such a hot climate, and almost as trying is the want of colour to refresh the eye. A few flowering aloes, and flowers of the order Solanaceæ or Atropaceæ are very abundant; but except in the depth of the rainy season when creepers abound everywhere, there is not much other floral display. Orchids, though far from uncommon, are unobtrusive in the localities they select, and very quiet in appearance. There is, in fact, nothing of that wealth and brilliancy of colour that one naturally associates with the tropics. Most of the hills are covered with short trees, amongst which acacias predominate, whilst gigantic baobobs stand out prominently here and there. The larger trees, amongst which the fig-sycamores are the most conspicuous, prefer the plains, especially the sides of the streams. It is here, too, that the ebony-tree is so abundant, and in some districts the indiarubber-tree. Higher up, the brush and scrub are usually very close and well interspersed with thorn bushes bearing thorns from one to three inches long, a quite impenetrable thicket in many places except to knife and hatchet. It is in these hillside fastnesses that the wild beasts repose by day, and, except when pressed by hunger, rarely leave them until the sun has set, and the short twilight has been followed by the dim light of the stars, or the more brilliant but by no means exposing light of even a tropical moon. The leopards especially have the credit of selecting these hillside fastnesses for their lairs : a fact referred to by Solomon, 'Come with me from the lions' dens, from the mountains of the leopards.' The district around and near Mpwapwa, and, I believe, all along the range, abounds in lion, leopard, hyena, rhinoceros, elephant, giraffe, buffalo, zebra, antelope, eland, gazelle, monkey, wild boar, porcupine, coney, jackal, serval, genet, mongoose, civet cat, and other small carnivora. In the small lakes near and among the hills there are also hippopotamus and crocodile.

In the frequent visits which at one time I used to pay to Kisokwe, a village seven miles from Mpwapwa, where I was living, I had to walk five miles across a plain, three of the miles being along a well-worn caravan path through the jungle. Going by night it was a rare thing to see wild animals except hyenas, as they all seem to shun proximity to man; but, returning in the morning, my native boy often showed me the tracks of the different animals which had crossed our path the night before. It was some time before I learned to distinguish the different footprints myself, and to the last I could not recognise them with anything like the facility which the natives showed in doing it.

The hyenas are the animals most frequently seen and heard. Sometimes they can be heard soon after sunset, and they whine at intervals through the night. About three in the morning the whining becomes more frequent, and alters in character; they are calling to each other to go home, the natives say. Then it becomes more and more distant, and finally ceases; and the hyenas have returned to their homes before the first rays of the dawn. I never so fully realised before the description in the Psalms: 'Thou makest darkness and it is night, wherein all the beasts of the forests do creep forth. The young lions roar after their prey, and seek their meat from God. The sun ariseth; they get them away, and lay them down in their dens. Man goeth forth unto his work, and to his labour until the evening.' This last sentence exactly describes one's hours in Central Africa. I frequently travelled by night to avoid the hot sun, yet rarely met a native. I only once went a long walk by night alone, though there is very little if any danger of being attacked, the wild beasts have such a dread of man. I suppose it is that man's original dominion over animals still survives to a large extent 'over every living thing that moveth upon the earth.' I have heard that a variety of leopard sometimes attacks man; but could hear of no instance of it. Also that the man-eating lion does; if so, he certainly is a rarity in Central Africa. A rogue buffalo certainly does occasionally, like one that attacked a friend of mine, Mr. Cole, of Kisokwe. But even this instance can hardly be quoted as an unprovoked attack, as the animal in question certainly had its privacy rudely intruded upon. The people at Kisokwe were in great want of meat, and Cole had gone out one evening hoping to be able to bring home some game. After searching for some time he saw an antelope at a distance, and commenced to stalk it. Being an accomplished hunter, he succeeded in getting well within range without attracting the animal's attention; but in doing so he executed a feat which must be almost unparalleled in the annals of hunting. So cautiously did he approach through the long grass that he was unnoticed by a buffalo lying down in it; and so intent was he on his expected game, that, unknown to himself, he stalked right up to the buffalo, and stood just in front of its head, with his back to it. In a second the astonished animal was on its feet, and the sound brought Cole sharply round; but so close were the two, that although Cole's gun was at full-cock, before he could shoot the buffalo had caught him on the back, and he and his gun parted company as they went flying through the air. A second and a third time did the infuriated animal gore and toss him before he could realise his position and restrain his shouts. Then he lay motionless and quiet feigning death, but expecting every moment that he would be tossed again. However, the buffalo stood eyeing him for a few minutes; and then, half satisfied that its work was done, trotted off and stood again to watch its work at a short distance, finally disappearing in the jungle; whilst Cole's native boy, a frightened spectator of what had been happening, ran to the house two miles away, and brought assistance.

I think most people's respect for the king of beasts is very much diminished when they come to live in his neighbourhood. When you come across one, he almost invariably makes off, and it is safer to let him go, unless you are a very true shot, or have several armed natives with you, as a wounded lion is a dangerous animal to deal with.

I remember Herr Krieger, the German in command of the furthest station in the interior, coming, one day, very unexpectedly upon a lion. He was shooting quail, and had just emptied both barrels and started in pursuit of a wounded bird. In the pursuit he jumped into a shallow pit or trench, and as he did so, a terrified lioness, who had been enjoying a nap, jumped out and disappeared. He was relieved to see her go, as his gun was unloaded.

A friend of mine told me that, on one of his marches, he came upon a lion a short distance from the path. One of the men went off to have a shot at it, which only irritated the animal, who pursued him with great leaps and bounds, as he rushed shouting back to the caravan; but on getting nearer the body of men, the lion evidently considered discretion the better part of valour, and acted accordingly.

In South Africa and in the North there are, I believe, man-eating lions; but in Central Africa I doubt if such exist. I never came across a single authentic instance of one, though I frequently made inquiries for the purpose of ascertaining the truth or falsehood of the stories I had heard on the subject. Occasionally I heard of a village being depopulated by lions, but the depopulating process always turned out to be not such a bloody affair as it sounded. On one occasion we camped in such a depopulated, deserted village. I asked some natives belonging to the place, who happened to be passing that day, how many of their people the lions had killed?

'None,' they replied.

'But I thought the lions had driven you from here?'

'Yes,' was the answer; 'they came every night and eat our cows and goats, and we were being starved out, so we had to go elsewhere.'

On another occasion I was camping with my wife and child on the banks of the Rocky River. It was a brilliant moonlight night, and our donkeys were tied up in the open village, which was not stockaded. Towards midnight a lion stalked them from the hills. He came past our tent within a few yards of it, and was nearly within reach of them, when they scented him, and at once began to roar, as only frightened donkeys can, and woke the men. The lion, alarmed at his approach being made such a public matter, turned tail and disappeared in the jungle. Next night we tied up the donkeys in a clearing in the jungle outside the village—a very exposed, unprotected spot—in hopes that the lion would give us a chance of shooting him; but his majesty was not to be tempted; so we saw no more of him.

A good donkey is an easy match for a hyena or a leopard, and can with safety be left outside at nights in districts where there are no lions. A leopard knows well that a donkey, like an English football player, is generally a good kick, and prefers to give him a wide berth; but a lion has the courage to attack a donkey though not quite in the style one gathers from story books. In them, the lion is supposed to march up to the donkey, give him a pat on his back, and then eat him. But a donkey has a soul above being patted on the back by a lion or any other animal, and if a lion offered to do so, would most certainly kick him in the ribs.

One night at a village near me, a lion killed a donkey belonging to a friend of mine, leaving most of the body. Next night my friend prepared to sit up in a tree and shoot him when he came to finish the body; so shortly after dusk he went with a candle to a selected tree close to the donkey's remains, whilst his men followed with his guns. Just as he reached the spot, there was his majesty commencing his evening meal. The guns were a short distance behind, so my friend could not shoot him; whilst the lion, catching sight of him, disappeared as quickly as he could. The lion had returned earlier than my friend expected; but perhaps lions always return soon after dusk to save their prey from the hyenas, as they cannot climb like leopards, and so like them place their unfinished prey for safety in the tops of the trees. It was in the top of a tree in my garden, that one morning I found the remains of a pet terrier, which had been left in my care. It was my custom to leave the terrier loose at nights, and he slept on the veranda with my mastiffs, no leopard or hyena daring to approach a little dog so befriended. But having taken the mastiffs to a village some distance off, at which I was staying for the night, I ordered the terrier to be shut up in an outhouse for safety. Unfortunately he broke loose in the night, and ran to his accustomed place on the veranda, where the leopard, finding him alone, seized the opportunity to carry him off and kill him. Next night four of us sat up in some broken-down huts round the tree, and waited for him. Soon after midnight we heard a tin bowl rattling on the veranda some hundred yards away, and guessed that the leopard was looking to see if there was another unprotected dog. Finding nothing, he evidently made for the tree at once, as presently we heard a grunt in the cassava plantation between our huts and the house, and in another moment a fine leopard appeared at the foot of the tree. He gave one look at a large trap which we had placed in his way, decided that it was not intended for him, and clearing a second trap eight feet up the tree, at one bound landed amongst the upper branches. We now rushed out from our hiding-places, and surrounded the tree; but it was a minute or two before we could get a shot at him, as, the moment a gun was aimed at him, he dodged round to the other side of the trunk; but he could not avoid four guns, and very soon he paused for a second to decide what next to do, and, as he did so, two bullets through his heart brought him to the ground.

One evening, on my first journey up-country, as I was stopping at a mission-station, my boy had carelessly chained up my mastiffs on the veranda at dusk instead of taking them straight to the outhouse as he ought to have done; for they were young then, and were not left to look after themselves at night. Suddenly a leopard, who had evidently smelt dog from below, and no doubt expected to find one of the half-starved little native dogs which abound everywhere, jumped up in between them. There he stood, perfectly motionless with surprise, on his first introduction to the British mastiff. He was not left long to decide what to do; for one dog got him by the head, the other by the tail, and the two quickly bowled him over. He lay perfectly still, astonished at the unexpected turn which events had taken; whilst the dogs, evidently puzzled at his quiet behaviour, simply held him there and growled, but offered him no further violence. Before the men who had been standing near could return with their guns, the leopard had taken advantage of the dogs' indecision to suddenly wriggle away and disappear in the darkness, leaving them without even a scratch.

A leopard will risk a good deal to get a dog, but a kid he seems quite unable to resist. A friend told me that one once jumped into his kitchen through the window after dawn, and pulled out a kid. At the same station whilst I was there another burst open the door of the hut in which two of the mission-men were sleeping, caught up a little kid that was just inside, and hastily retreated. I see now the force of associating these two animals in the verse, 'The leopard shall lie down with the kid.'

One moonlight night I saw a leopard stalk his prey. He had crept up the long garden to behind an aloe, a few yards from where a puppy was sleeping close to the window of my bedroom. He was ready for his final spring, when the mastiff, who was hidden in the shade, caught sight of him; and a second later the leopard was tearing down the garden with the mastiff a few feet from his tail. However, he outran the dog, and escaped over the fence.

Leopards are such very cunning animals that it is by no means easy to successfully snare or shoot them. They are more cunning by far than hyenas; but their habit of skulking about buildings and outhouses at dusk in search of prey, and their confidence in their own powers of eluding capture by cunning or rapidity of movement, brings them in far closer contact with their human enemy, and consequently they are more often killed or captured than the less cunning, but far more shy and timid, hyena.

I remember seeing a trap set by a friend of mine for a leopard. He had built a hut of very strong timberwork interwoven with thorns; and leaving the door of this open, he placed a steel trap under the doorway quite concealed by grass and leaves. In the hut an inviting young kid was tied up, who soon attracted the leopard by his bleating when night began. The leopard, however, contrary to expectation, declined to enter by the door, which he evidently considered lay open in a suspiciously ostentatious manner, but instead, with his powerful paws smashed through the walls of the hut, howling aloud all the time with the pain caused by the thorns, yet persevering until he had made a sufficient opening by which to withdraw the kid, when he instantly made off with his booty.

It is useless to endeavour to kill a leopard by exposing poisoned meat, as he will not be tempted by food which he has not killed himself; but he may be poisoned, none the less, by a method which some German colonists near us devised. A kid was very firmly tied up near the house, and left out for the night. Before long his violent bleating and struggles disclosed the fact that he was being attacked; whereupon a rush was made for the place with lights, and sure enough his mangled body was found not yet wrenched away from its fastenings by the leopard which had killed him. Strychnine was then well rubbed into the wounds, and the body left; and next morning the body of the leopard was found close to the carcase of the kid, which bore traces of having been still further mangled, and partially devoured.

Another plan is to tie up a goat at night near a window which is in the shade, and wait for the leopard; but he will not approach on a moonlight night, whilst on a moonless starlit one it is very difficult to follow his rapid movements. The whole matter is over in one or two seconds—one bound brings the leopard out of the darkness, and a few seconds suffice him to kill the goat, and wrench as much of it away as he dare stay for, with the odour of the hidden watcher so perceptibly strong—hardly time for the watcher to collect his wits, especially if he has been watching for several hours.

But the most satisfactory plan is a gun-trap set in the track of the animal at night, when the blackened string becomes quite invisible.

Hyenas are so wary of approaching man that it is difficult to get a shot at them. Almost the only occasions are when you come suddenly upon them when walking through the jungle on a moonlight night. Even then one needs to be a very good shot to hit them before they have disappeared. Several times I have come upon them suddenly in this way, but usually when I had no gun. Once I was riding through the jungle at dusk, when three hyenas—who had evidently smelt the donkey, but not me—jumped out on to the path a few yards ahead. I felt very uncomfortable, as I had no gun, and did not then know the habits of these animals. They quickly disappeared when they discovered that there was a man as well as a donkey; but I could hear them howling near for some time after, and I

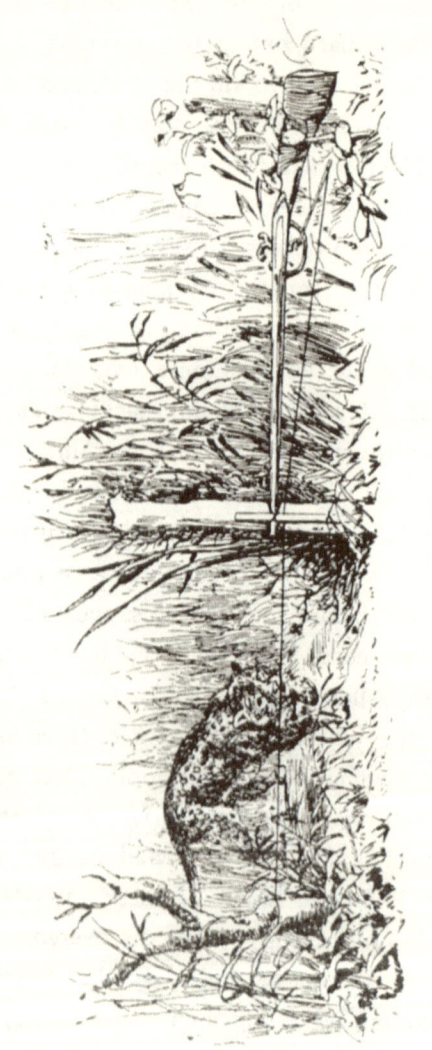

GUN-TRAP

was not sorry when I found myself safe back in my own compound.

Though not easily shot, troublesome hyenas can usually be got rid of by poisoning. Any garbage rubbed with strychnine will answer the purpose. Unless the dead body used is a large one, it is necessary to fasten it securely, as by nailing it to a tree, otherwise the hyena will carry off the tempting morsel to devour it at his leisure in his own home, and so his skin will be lost, and there will not even be the certainty that he has been killed. On one occasion I exposed some goat's meat, well rubbed with strychnine, to get rid of some civet cats who were paying our hen-roosts nightly visits. The first morning after, the meat was found gnawed, and the dead body of a civet cat close by. The next morning the meat was again found gnawed, and the marks were those of a small carnivor, but no civet cat could be found, though the amount eaten left no doubt that the animal must have died close by, and probably had been carried off by a hyena, who in his turn would also have died, but at a distance, as the poison was in a diluted form; so we searched for his body, but without result, until after a few days the progress of decomposition caused an odour which betrayed its position, not only to us, but also a night or two later to some other hyenas, who thereupon made a meal of the remains of their brother, but whether or no with fatal results, I never ascertained.

Nearly all the injuries from wild animals that I saw whilst in Africa were caused by hyenas. These animals prowl around every camp, and if they come upon a man asleep away from his camp fire, will at once pounce upon him, secure one mouthful—and a very satisfying mouthful it usually is—and rush away. I remember one hot night while a number of boys were sleeping on the veranda of a Mission House, a hyena came in and seized one of the smallest boys by his elbow, and was making off with him, when with great presence of mind he raised the war-cry. At once others came to his rescue, and he was saved, but not before his elbow-bones had been torn out. However, he made a very good recovery. Another time a boy was brought to me who was suffering from small-pox, and who whilst in this condition, lying in some exposed place at night, had his ankle badly crushed by a bite from the same powerful jaws; and I have occasionally seen people with part of their cheeks or their ears gone.

Cowardly though they are, hyenas will sometimes follow alone behind people at night in the hope that they will lie down. They are said sometimes to follow, walking for short distances at a time on their hind legs, and I believe this is really the case. On one occasion I was walking unarmed at night from a native servant's house to my own, a distance of about fifty yards. As I walked down the sloping path I heard bare feet come pattering after me, and, turning round, said, to what I supposed was the servant, 'What do you want, Richard?' My heart stood still, as the only answer I received was the sound of a jump made by some large animal, and a plunge and crash into the bushes by the side of the stream, close to which I was walking. The animal was probably a hyena; had it been a leopard it would have slunk off more quietly.

The hyenas are occasionally called wolves by travellers, but there are no wolves in Central Africa. Hyenas, jackals, and hunting-dogs, especially the latter, take their place. The hunting-dogs are large dogs that hunt in packs, and when pressed by hunger will, it is said, attack even man. Certainly they will do so in self-defence. Their method of hunting is very interesting. Having scented their game, perhaps an antelope, they surround him in a large circle and gradually close in upon him, taking advantage of every bit of cover that offers itself to keep out of his sight. Presently he discovers one of his enemies, and at once prepares to make off in an opposite direction, when a sharp bark immediately in front of him pulls him suddenly up, and an attempt to alter his course and escape by another way is checked in the same manner. At last he gets frantic, and makes a rush, unheeding the barks in front of him; but by this time the whole circle have closed in, and one or two have got their fangs into him. He shakes them off; they have delayed, not stopped him, and he rushes away again; but the delay has given time for others to get ahead of him, and again he is seized, and again, until finally he succumbs to his many enemies, who in an hour will have left nothing of him but his larger bones for the hyenas who will scour the ground that night.

I never once saw a hippopotamus or rhinoceros, but occasionally came across the tracks of the latter. The natives are much afraid of the rhinoceros; in fact, he and the solitary buffalo are far more dreaded than the lion, as these do occasionally attack man unprovoked, though as a rule, they are not very formidable foes, and with care can be hunted without any great danger. The rhinoceros is chiefly hunted for its horns, the buffalo for both skin and horns, as the natives make sandals, which are much

ANTELOPE, HUNTED BY DOGS.

prized for their toughness, out of buffalo-hide. The hippopotamus is hunted more especially for its teeth, many tons of which are annually sent to Europe, and there sold as an inferior quality of ivory for knife-handles and suchlike purposes. The hippopotamus is generally trapped, a heavily-weighted spear being suspended over its run, and a cord so arranged across the path, that when it is displaced by the foot of the animal, the spear is released, and plunges into its back, the animal going off not far away to die from the bleeding, which enables the hunter who has set the trap to track his victim to its death-place.

Elephants roam the forests in many districts, but they seem to be most plentiful north-east of Uganda, in the district first explored by Count Teleky, so that the best hunting-ground and the approaches to it are now in the hands of the Imperial British East Africa Company. A hunter, who lived on Lake Nyassa, told me that the natives about there go out in parties of about twenty armed with old muskets to hunt the elephant. Having sighted their game, they cautiously creep up to within a few yards of him, and then, all firing together, give him a regular broadside. But the aim is so bad, and the penetration of their missiles so feeble, that the elephant usually escapes with nothing worse than a dozen skin-wounds. In the districts where I have lived, poisoned arrows are always used in elephant-hunting; but I could not find out exactly what was the poison used; apparently it was a mixture of several ingredients, which included cobra poison and some vegetable extract.

The teeth of the African elephant are so different from those of the Indian species, that I was very much surprised one day in the interior to come upon some teeth which undoubtedly came from the Indian. The phenomenon was explained soon after by discovering that the Belgian expedition into the interior of Africa had been supplied with elephants as carriers by the Indian Government, and had lost one of them by death at this place.

Antelope are the most common of all the beasts of the field, from the graceful, tiny gazelle, no larger than an Italian greyhound, to the splendid sikiro, or koodoo, as he is called in South Africa, as large as a good-sized horse. They used to come into our garden every night, and it was some time before I recognised their cry, which is so like the loud deep bark of a large dog, that most Europeans mistake it for that at first.

Monkeys are to be seen by thousands, but they

keep so cunningly hidden amongst the foliage, that it takes a stranger some time to discover them. He may live there for some months hardly seeing one, and suddenly he will learn where to look for them, and will see them perhaps every day after that. They were a great nuisance in the garden when the maize began to ripen; whole troops constantly invaded the place, one monkey being always sent to occupy a conspicuous place, from which he gave timely warning to the others of the approach of danger; he never joined himself in collecting the spoil, so I supposed that the native statement, that he receives his share afterwards, must be correct.

An animal allied to the monkey which is fairly plentiful, but on account of its nocturnal habits, not often seen, is a variety of lemur, the loris, or potto, I am not sure which. Sir Charles Bell, in his Treatise on the Hand, says of this animal: ' It might be pitied for the slowness of its movements if these were not necessary to its very existence. It steals on its prey by night, and extends its arms towards the birds on the branch, or the great moth, with a motion so imperceptibly slow, as to make sure of its object.' He further adds: ' It may be well to notice some other characters that belong to animals, inhabitants of the tropical regions, which prowl by night. The various creatures that enliven the woods in the daytime in these warm climates have fine skins and smooth hair, but those that seek their prey at night have a thick coat like animals of the Arctic regions. What is this but to be clothed as the sentinel whose watch is in the night? They have eyes, too, which, from their peculiar structure, are called nocturnal, being formed to admit a large pencil of rays of light, and having the globe full and prominent, and the iris contractile, to open the pupil to the greatest extent.'*

Wild boar seem obtainable everywhere, but not in large numbers. The natives shoot them for food, but the flesh is rather rank and very lean, and it is a little risky to eat it, as, unfortunately, it is often infested with *Trichinæ*, African hogs, as well as their European brethren, suffering from trichinosis.

Rats swarm everywhere, and are a great nuisance. They and the white ants give a housekeeper an anxious time. One day I went into the store-room to get a pot of honey, and found that two rats had eaten through the cover, and then gone in after the honey. They had got so sticky that they could not jump out again, and there they had apparently

---

* 'The Hand,' Sir Charles Bell, 9th edit., p. 22. London: George Bell and Son, York Street, Covent Garden, 1874.

remained for some days. I should think they must have been very thirsty. We always had the greatest difficulty in keeping our meat from them, until at last we hit upon a plan which baffled them. If we suspended the meat from the roof by wire, they slid down the wire. If we hung it on wire stretched tightly across the room, they managed to swarm along the wire; but we were successful when we hung the meat by a rope and made a knot in the rope halfway down, which just stopped a sheet of tin with a central hole in it. The rats came down the rope as far as the tin sheet, and there they stopped. If they endeavoured to get on to the tin, it tilted on one side with their weight, and being too slippery for them to cling to, they fell to the ground, just clear of the meat.

Central Africa is very rich in different species of birds, especially along the great mountain chain. The two most noticeable families are perhaps the hawks and shrikes. Hawks and kites are frequently seen hovering overhead in search of the smaller birds and mammals which crowd the undergrowth. As a rule they soar out of reach of shot, and it is not easy to hit a flying bird with a bullet. They will soar for hours at this provoking distance, and then suddenly swoop down upon your pets or your poultry, and carry them off before you can get within range. Even when near, it is not always easy to bring them down with shot. I have before now fired straight up at a hawk overhead with a charge of pellets, and broken its legs; but it still flew on in circles as if nothing had happened, with legs hanging down limp and useless.

The brilliant plumaged shrikes which meet the eye everywhere are in great number, and in great variety; corresponding to the incredible profusion of insects which crowd hill, dale and moor of Central Africa, and upon which they live. But for the shrikes, no agriculturalist would save any of his crop, and even the woods would soon be laid bare. Brilliantly coloured though the shrikes are, the sun-birds and plantain-eaters quite outshine them. The sun-birds are the representatives in Africa of the humming-birds of America. They have the same gorgeous plumage, the same long curved bill for sucking the honey out of flowers, and the same elegant diminutive figure, though not quite so diminutive as their American sisters. The plantain-eaters on the contrary are rather larger in size than a pigeon. Their plumage is in varying shades of one colour, lavender, purple or olive green being the most common, with, in each case, a broad band of bright red across the wings. On the head is a large and elegant crest of feathers. The eyes and eyelids are a deep orange. They are birds of indifferent powers of flight, usually flying only from one tree to a neighbouring one, alighting on one of the lower branches, and hopping gradually up to the highest, from which they fly to the next tree, and so on. It is a little difficult to shoot them with anything except pellets, as they are screened very much by the boughs and foliage until they reach the summit of a tree, when they are usually out of reach of ordinary shot, which will not kill at such an elevation. These birds are easily recognised at a distance by their peculiar cry, which exactly resembles the name given to them by the natives—the kulu-kulu. Some of the interior tribes use their wings as head ornaments; but it is said that no one is allowed to wear them unless he has distinguished himself by killing a man in battle.

There are several varieties of king-fisher, even in the districts where there are no fish; but even there they frequent the tiny streams and feed on the insects which specially abound amongst the copious vegetation on the banks.

The immense swarms of bees which inhabit Africa naturally bring the bee-eaters in great numbers to these regions. Starlings of brighter plumage than our European ones abound everywhere, and so do finches of different varieties. The Whydah finch is very conspicuous. A small bird with two feathers in its tail, about the size of those from the tail of a full-sized cock. This finch can easily be recognised at a distance by the two long feathers streaming out behind, which greatly impede its flight, giving it a very up and down movement. It always flies accompanied by half a dozen or more females, of duller plumage, and lacking the long tail feathers. It is a polygamous bird, I believe the only finch guilty of such a habit.

The roller bird, which looks like a jay, and has much the same habits, is a very conspicuous object in the woods; and so is the hoopoo with its elegant spreading crest. A group of these latter birds with their fluffy plumage and short fluttering flight looks not unlike a swarm of gigantic moths. Then there are two or three varieties of swallow, which build mud nests like our own variety; but the European swallow, which arrives on the great plateau at the end of November, and leaves at the end of February, builds no nest, and consequently has always been a source of surprise to the natives, who wondered where it went to in the summer, and why it built no nest; the prevalent idea being that it hid in holes during that period. It is not so long since in England the popular idea was that the swallows hibernated in holes during the winter, and in many country places the belief still exists.

HORNBILL

The huge ungainly-looking greater hornbills, which are not infrequently seen in pairs, do not look so out of place amongst the baobob trees. Whatever the traveller may think of the ungainliness of baobob trees and hornbills, he must feel that the design of the one is in perfect harmony with that of the other. The smaller hornbills are of great frequency everywhere. The bird certainly does not live upon garbage or small animals as some books state, but chiefly upon fruits and nuts. It is stated that it can feed with impunity upon *nux vomica*, the nut from which strychnine is extracted; but I was never able to ascertain if this statement was correct or not.

The cuckoo appears to be common all over Africa, but the Central African variety is certainly indigenous, the European variety not visiting these regions as the swallow does. In shape and plumage the African bird very closely resembles its English relative; but the cry is quite different. 'Tip-tip' betrays its presence from quite a distance, and the natives name it after its cry, a very usual custom amongst the nature-observing Africans, some of whom call the jackal 'mbwehe,' and the cat 'miaou.' The natives assured me that the cuckoo builds nests like other birds, and though they could never show me a specimen, I expect they were correct, as they are very close observers of the habits of birds and animals.

The Weaver bird is very plentiful, and its elegantly

woven nest is the most conspicuous object in many of the trees. But though conspicuous and exposed, the nest is fairly safe from enemies. The bird invariably builds upon a thorn-tree, and usually at the very end of one of its branches; the nest, light though it is, dragging down the frail twig by its weight. No man or carnivor dare climb far up into this inhospitable tree; and even the smaller monkeys, though they might reach within a couple of yards of the nest, dare not take the final spring into the fine network of terrible thorns that lie between them and their coveted booty. From hawks, most of the nests are protected by their tunnel-shaped entrance; whilst the few that are constructed without this protecting tunnel, and so more exposed, I have noticed, are built side by side with a hornets' nest, which the natives told me was the usual arrangement. Any large bird disturbing the branches around the nest would at the same time disturb the hornets, who would make short work of the intruder.

Towards dusk the night-jars appear on the paths, and seem to fly up from under your very feet; whilst, when darkness has quite set in, the owls commence their melancholy hooting, which they keep up at intervals during the night. I never succeeded in getting a specimen of an owl. It is very difficult to discover their exact whereabouts; and the natives consider it unlucky to shoot them, so that they never would bring me one.

In such a wooded country as Africa, of course wood-peckers abound, and the tap, tap of their beaks against the hollow trees can often be heard half a mile away.

Guinea-fowl, quail, pigeons and doves are the chief edible birds. Guinea-fowl are very abundant, and very good eating. Doves, also, are common enough in the woods, and always obtainable; but pigeons are not so plentiful, and I have only seen one variety wild—a bird with a large excrescence of purple skin at the base of its beak, and with slaty blue plumage. Tame pigeons, of several varieties, are common in the villages; they have gradually extended by barter from Zanzibar, to which they were sent from Europe, I believe.

The natives are very ingenious in the construction of complicated traps for the capture of birds; I have often stopped to examine the system of levers and springs constructed with flexible twigs, and with strips of bark as ligatures. I unfortunately did not make a drawing of any, and they were too intricate to be recalled to mind without. The boys often capture birds by smearing a kind of bird-lime on the leaves and twigs of the bushes they frequent.

Reptiles naturally abound in such a tropical climate as that of Eastern Equatorial Africa. Snakes are everywhere seen, from the tiny grass snake, like a piece of narrow green ribbon, to the splendid python, thirty or more feet long. Yet snakes in Africa must be far more sluggish in their habits than those in India. At Mpwapwa, where I lived for a year in a village of perhaps two thousand people, there was only one case of snake bite, and that not a fatal one; although we often came across snakes, the puff-adder in turning over stones, and cobras in the rooms or outhouses at night. The African cobra does not raise itself so high as the Indian one when about to strike; rarely more than eight or nine inches; neither does it inflate its hood so widely. I discovered a cobra once at night in a hut near our dwelling, and as I was not a very good shot, I went up close to it before firing; but only succeeded in cutting its tail off. My friend, who was a very good shot, but unsteady from an attack of fever, was anxious that I should not shoot again, as he wanted the head uninjured. So he took the gun and aimed. 'I will spare the head,' he said; and fired. When the smoke cleared away, we found that he had spared the head and apparently the body, too, as the creature was gone. Another time I was waked up at night by the noise of what I thought was a rat after some biscuits, which were on a table near; and I tried to hit the creature, whatever it might be, with a slipper, when a horrid hissing noise warned me to desist; so I struck a light and took my gun from its usual place at the bedside, whilst my wife went to fetch the boy. Presently he came, and then he pulled away a box behind which the creature was, whilst I fired at it, as its hiding-place was exposed. The cobras come into houses usually in search of rats. We had previously noticed that there had been a great scarcity of rats in the house for some weeks; but we did not then know enough of the ways of cobras to guess the reason. On another occasion one of the boys discovered a cobra in an outhouse behind some boxes; but he did not at the time know that it was a large snake. He fired at it, but only succeeded in wounding it. When I came, I managed to spear it about eighteen inches from the tail, and as I supposed, close to its head; as we failed, however, to get it out, we thought we would tie a string to its tail, and then releasing the spear from the floor, to which it pinned the animal, pull it out, and despatch it. We tied the string on very tightly, trusting to the animal being speared close to the head to prevent its turning upon us. But on loosening the spear, and pulling the animal out by the long string, we were surprised to find a six-foot cobra, which had been speared close to its tail, and which, consequently, might at any moment have turned upon us whilst we were tying it. It sounds rather like a story from the 'Lays of Ind,' to talk of tying strings on cobras' tails, and so pulling them out of their hiding-places. But snakes in Central Africa are far less savage than people at home suppose.

I never saw a really large python. The largest I came across measured about fourteen feet. It was killed by a native near our house after it had made a meal off seven of his fowls.

Lizards meet you at almost every turn in the path as you walk along; little creatures most of them, about the size of a newt or smaller. Some varieties live in the houses, running up the walls; and, what looks very curious, along the ceilings, too, after moths and other insects. They stalk their tiny prey very carefully and very patiently. A lightning dash forwards is followed by a few seconds of absolutely motionless repose; then another dash, and yet another, until they are near enough to make their final rush, which is usually successful; though they frequently fail in getting their prey, as the insect generally makes off before they are near enough to make the final rush. There are large lizards, too; but these are rarer, some being more than a foot long, adorned with the most brilliant scarlet colouring, and having stumpy tails that look just as if they had been bitten off short.

Chameleons are far from uncommon; but they stand so motionless on the twigs amongst the foliage, and adapt their colour so rapidly to their surroundings, that only an experienced eye discovers them. The rapidity with which they change colour is very surprising. I have seen one change in less than a minute from a yellow and brown to a most delicate transparent green, exactly like the young leaves of the banana-tree on which it stood. The natives told me that tobacco-juice would kill the chameleon almost instantly. I expressed incredulity; whereupon they gave one a little piece of tobacco which they had fixed on the end of a stick, and heated in the fire until it exuded its sticky juice. The chameleon snapped angrily at the tobacco, and then marched on slowly as if nothing had happened, a fact which I pointed out to the natives. 'Wait a little, master, wait and see,' they replied. The chameleon had hardly gone twenty steps when it began to stagger, stopped short, and then gradually began to shake all over, as if it had a violent attack of St. Vitus' dance. Slowly its sides sank in, its

THE MANTIS

limbs were drawn towards its body, its tail curled up, and it fell over on its side dead.

The curious insects which mimic in shape and colour sticks, leaves, and other inanimate objects, have been very accurately described by Professor

Drummond in his book on 'Tropical Africa,' as have also the white ants. I differ so widely from him in his accounts of the people and the climatic diseases that I am glad to be able to bear testimony to his descriptions of trees and animals, which are no less accurately than they are charmingly told.

The butterflies are neither so varied nor so gorgeous as one would have expected; but their comparative scarcity and sombreness are in keeping with the character of the vegetation. Beetles, on the other hand, are both beautiful and numerous. Central Africa is a paradise for the entomologist who devotes himself to beetles. Grasshoppers of every size swarm and make a continuous din all day long in the depths of the woods and everywhere at dusk, when the sound is sometimes quite deafening. Ants of every variety swarm on the ground. One kind called 'siafu' march in compact columns an inch or two wide, and many yards in length. Their bite is rather severe, so that it is no joke to step unconsciously on such a column. On a caravan journey the traveller will cross two or three of these columns every day. The leading man looks out for them, and, as he sees them, the word 'siafu' passes rapidly from front to rear of the caravan, and everyone is on the look-out for them. They occasionally enter the houses, and I have more than once been turned out of bed at midnight by them; and they sometimes gave us trouble by getting into our fowl-yard or goat-pen. The poor animals' cries used to wake us up, and we had to go and hold torches to the front of the column of ants and burn them by thousands before we could persuade them to alter their course. Their invasion of a house is not by any means an unmitigated evil. Through it they make their irresistible march, and clean the place for you as no effort of your own could clean it. Every insect, be it moth or mosquito, beetle or cockroach, is quickly covered, and as quickly eaten, not a white ant remains to tell the tale of the invasion; even the lizards are picked clean to the bones, and the very scorpions in their apparently impregnable armour have to succumb to the onslaughts of such unnumbered foes. A very few hours usually suffices to take the column through, and leave you with a clean house, though perhaps an empty larder.

Scorpions are very numerous, especially in sandy rocky districts, as Ugogo, where the vast plains covered with loose stones give unlimited cover to both scorpions and puff-adders. The scorpions vary from one to eight or more inches in length. I believe their sting is occasionally dangerous; but I have never known it cause more than transient pain and swelling. Bees do far more damage than scorpions; but then they are, of course, more useful. The natives hollow out logs for them or utilize the empty packing-cases left by passing caravans,* which they place amongst the branches of the trees. These you see perched up in the trees all about, each with its swarm of bees. When the honey season comes, the boxes are lowered at night into a fire of dry grass, the bees destroyed, and the honey taken. Occasionally the bees seem to get fits of anger, and buzz furiously around their hives, descending on any bird, animal, or man who happens to pass beneath at the time. Some were kept in the loft of a house of a friend with whom I was staying; and once, when they were angry, they came down and killed a tame eagle belonging to my friend, whilst on another occasion they killed a small monkey which I had bought as entomological attendant for my dogs.

Amidst all this teeming animal life, and the

* Tate's cube-sugar boxes are such a very convenient size for loads, that they are largely used as packing-cases for goods sent by caravan, and find their last resting-places in the trees of Central Africa. Mr. Tate is more widely advertised than he imagines.

Disposal of Refuse

luxuriant undergrowth in the rainy season, what becomes of the refuse is a question that naturally occurs to the traveller who sees the ground so bare and with such scanty remains of death or decay. A large animal, say an antelope, dies in the morning; what becomes of the body? Before an hour has passed, flies in large numbers will have settled upon it, and laid, not eggs, but living maggots, which will be seen revelling in the juices of the eye, and along the free borders of the lips.* Later in the day the body will have been seen by crows and hawks, who will swoop down and help themselves to the eyes, and occasionally to some of the viscera. As night draws on, the body, if near a regular hyenas' beat, will be scented by these animals; if off their beat, it will remain untouched until sufficiently decomposed to attract their attention from a distance. I have seen a man's body lie three days in an unfrequented ravine before being scented by the

---

* These flies are the bane of dwellers in the tropics, and are the cause of meat turning so quickly. But we found that in the hottest season we could keep meat for forty-eight hours, if directly the animal was killed it was cut up neatly into joints, and these dried on the surface by dusting a little flour over and hung up in a shady airy place, enclosed in large loose bags of fine muslin, which effectually prevented the entrance of these flies, as well as of the minuter kinds which were able to pass through mosquito-netting.

hyenas. But this state of things is unusual; and the first night the hyenas and jackals usually satisfy themselves with the viscera and some of the soft parts, returning on the second night to dispose of the rest, bones and all, leaving only some of the skull, which even their jaws are unable to crack. Meanwhile, the maggots which commenced operations the first hour continue their work upon the brain, and in other secluded spots, until the sun so dries up their food that they are no longer able to make any impression upon it. The siafu now come upon the scene, and gnaw away every dry fragment of flesh which has resisted the efforts of the softer-feeding maggots, who themselves go to form a relish to the harder food if they have been imprudent enough to linger behind after the advent of the siafu. The contents of the alimentary canal which have escaped being swallowed with the viscera are now carefully collected by the scavenger beetles, rolled into little balls, and carried off to their homes. The larger pieces of dry skin, too extensive or too sun-dried for the siafu, are left for the wire-worms, which soon demolish every fragment. It is these little creatures which are the dread of taxidermists, and by their proclivities make such havoc amongst his treasures.

In like manner the immense profusion of dead vegetable matter, the millions of decayed trees and fallen boughs, directly they are thoroughly dry are attacked by a small grub—the so-called 'white ant,' the larva of an insect allied to the dragon-fly. The white ants inhabit every acre of tropical Africa in countless billions, and never leave over from one year to the other any fragment of dead dry wood; all is consumed, and so turned into soil. Professor Drummond observes truly that they do the work of the worms of more temperate regions. But worms are plentiful, none the less, even in tropical Africa, though their work is confined to the few weeks when the ground is sufficiently soft for them to perform their functions.

Thus every remnant of refuse is removed from the soil; and notwithstanding the profusion of vegetation in the rainy season, and the abundance of animal life, no refuse long remains to taint the air, or encumber the ground of the unfrequented, uncultivated, and uninhabited jungles of Central Africa.

CHAPTER III

THE PEOPLE

For many years past, the peoples whose habitat is, roughly speaking, Africa south of the equator—a district of some four and a half million square miles, with a population of over forty million—have been known to anthropologists and linguists by the name of 'Bantu,' a word meaning 'persons' in the dialect of one of the southern tribes of these peoples—the Kaffirs.

The branches of this great Bantu family speak dialects of one great language, entirely differing from any other language known to us, with the exception of those of Polynesia. The two chief peculiarities of this language are that all the grammatical changes, with hardly an exception, are produced by prefixes; and that the different parts of speech in a sentence are all made to agree with the principal noun by an alliterative change of prefix. The nouns are divided into classes, of which about

An Alliterative Language

half a dozen are in common use; and nearly every word in a sentence will require its prefix to be altered should the noun be changed or even altered from the singular to the plural. An example taken from the Swahili dialect will best make the matter clear:

> *Mtu mwema mmoja wa Sultani alianguka:*
> One good man of (the) Sultan fell.*
> *Watu wema wengi wa Sultani walianguka:*
> Many good men of (the) Sultan fell.
> *Vitu vyema vingi vya Sultani vilianguka:*
> Many good things of (the) Sultan fell.

In these three sentences nearly every word changes its prefix according to its agreement with mtu, *man;* watu, *men;* or vitu, *things.* It was these alliterative changes which made it so difficult for the first missionaries and explorers to get a grasp of the grammar of the language, and which led some of the earlier Jesuit missionaries to the Congo to describe it as an unintelligible language without a grammar.

Although the tribes south of 5° N. Lat. are almost entirely Bantu, there is a group of families which has intruded from the north-east, and which, limited on the west by the Victoria Nyanza, has spread southwards as far as 6° S. Lat. Of this group the

* Literally: Man good one of Sultan he did-fall.

Masai are the chief. Again, in the extreme south there is a tribe believed to be quite distinct from the Bantu, although living amongst them—viz., the Hottentots, or bushmen. These bushmen, who until lately were considered the most diminutive people in the world, are, I have little doubt, of the same race as the pigmies of Schweinfurth and Stanley. They are, it is true, rather taller than the pigmies; but this is easily explained by the more temperate climate in which they live—just as the Zulus, who live in the same latitude, are so much taller than their tropical Bantu brethren. A Zulu bears about the same proportion to an Mgogo that a bushman does to a pigmy. There is no reason why the bushmen or pigmies should not be found at intervals over the forest lands from the Cape to the equator; for even now the Zulus, in scattered bands, reach right to the equator—parties of warriors who fled from Zululand years ago from fear of Ketchwayo or his father. They are called Maviti in the equatorial district. They retain the Zulu language, but rather altered from that which is spoken in the south. With the exceptions mentioned above, all tribes within the limits named belong to one great family, and speak languages agreeing in grammar, and differing only in dialect in the different localities. The Congo people on the west coast, the Zulus and so-called Kaffirs in the south, the Swahili on the east coast, and the Waganda, or Buganda as they call themselves, all, therefore, belong to one family; and anyone who knows one of these languages will at once be able to pick up words here and there in a book written in any of the others, and will be familiar, of course, with the grammar of all. It is the great similarity of language which renders it possible for a traveller knowing only one language to pass from one side of Africa to the other, and which thus enabled Stanley and Cameron, knowing only Swahili, or Livingstone, knowing only Sechuana, to cross the Continent south of the equator.

The Bantu differs much from the typical negro. His hair is not so much like wool; occasionally it is even nearly straight. The colour of his skin is never so dark, but varies from a very dark brown to a shade scarcely darker than that of an Italian; and his features as a rule are much more chiselled and refined.

It is impossible to say which tribe are to be considered the purest Bantu, or what perhaps is the same thing, which speaks the dialect least altered from the original mother tongue. Yet it is generally admitted that it must be sought amongst the tribes south of the Orange River, possibly the so-called Kaffirs. In the north, undoubtedly the people and languages have both been altered by admixture with the races bordering upon them; the Swahili, in addition to these alterations, show traces of much admixture with the Arab and Hindu. Indeed the Swahili language has completely lost two of its numerals—'six' and 'seven': *mtandatu* and *mfungate* —their places being supplied by the Arabic *sita* and *saba*.

The ethnological feature most noticeable to the traveller, as he goes inland from the Swahili coast, is the small size of the tribes which he comes across, and the want of unity amongst the villages of each tribe. A chief near the coast seems rarely to rule over more than a thousand subjects, and one in the interior rarely over more than three thousand, usually very much fewer; whilst it is only here and there that chiefs are found owning any allegiance to a greater chief or overlord. This want of unity, and the evil that results from it, will be considered in the chapter on the slave-trade.

In beliefs and customs the various tribes have much in common. I always made a practice of inquiring from natives what they believed before I spoke to them about our own beliefs; but I never

Religious Beliefs

came across one who did not know that there was a God who created the world, and Who still exercised some kind of influence, more or less indefinite, over its welfare. Nor yet, strangely enough, did I ever come across one who believed in a future life, or to whom it had ever occurred that the grave or the hyenas were not his final destiny. Though with this belief there was a strangely inconsistent custom of propitiating the spirits of the deceased; building little huts for them, and placing within for their use a little food and a cooking utensil—food which the spirits of their relations, or the wild animals, did certainly carry away.

I was unable to discover much about any religious practice or ceremony amongst the East Africans in the interior. This was due partly to their shyness in speaking to a white man about their beliefs, partly to my inability to converse confidentially with them on account of my ignorance of any dialect beyond that used at the coast, and partly, no doubt, to the very hazy and indefinite nature of the ideas which they have on the subject. They seem to have some notion of ancestral worship, or rather worship of their progenitors whom they had known before death—a worship which I was unable to reconcile with their expressed disbelief in any future state.

One instance of sacrifice I did come across, when, towards the end of a long drought, a few natives went to a retired spot to pray for rain, and, as part of the ceremony, killed and cooked a goat 'for God,' they said, but they eat it themselves, notwithstanding.

Of abstract right and wrong they have some very distinct ideas, though these are very limited in number. For instance, they show their appreciation of the excellence of truthfulness by being very indignant if they are accused of lying, and to be called a thief is a mark of great reproach. The only idea of defilement that I could ascertain they possessed was amongst those tribes which drew strict lines of demarcation between women who were nearly related or allied to men, and those who were not, the former never being allowed to approach within a certain distance of their male relatives or clansmen, and the infraction of this rule causing defilement to the man. I never heard, however, of any ceremonial cleansing being rendered necessary by such defilement, and I think that the only ceremony resulting was a good beating administered to the unfortunate or incautious woman.

I never heard of an instance of idols being worshipped in East Africa, though charms or fetishes, as they are variously called, abound all across the Continent. The natives wear charms, suspend them over their doorways, place them in front of their thresholds, on their farms—in fact everywhere. They look upon these charms, or medicines as they call them, as good devices which will counteract the evil devices of men or supernatural beings. Charms, then, are the antidotes to witchcraft.

The leading idea of witchcraft is that one individual can, by incantations, or by compounding a mixture, cause his neighbour to fall ill or even to die, or he can afflict his live stock in a similar way. The individual so affected can, if he is aware of what has taken place, counteract these incantations or mixtures, either by more potent ones of his own, or by compassing the death of the author of them, as the death of a wizard is supposed to result in the neutralization of his charms. Now, sometimes these mixtures are actual poisons, and not only is this the case, but they are administered surreptitiously to the individual whom it is desired to bewitch; and in these cases of course the illness or death of the bewitched individual is the direct result of the wizard's mixtures. I was never able to ascertain what poisons were used, but was told that they were vegetable products. Possibly belladonna or nux vomica, as these plants are found in the interior. It is strange that though vegetable drugs are used for this purpose, and also for tipping arrows, yet they rarely, if ever, seem applied to the healing of disease. The only product that I could ascertain was made use of, was that from the castor oil tree; the fresh oil obtained from the nuts, or the juice expressed from the leaves, being used for external application, as a stimulant to breasts which refused to yield their proper supply of milk.

A native seeing an instance of people actually dying shortly after being bewitched, and being unaware of the part which poison had played in the matter, would not unnaturally conclude, by a hasty generalization, that all witchcraft had an equally sure result. His belief in witchcraft is a logical not a moral, a mental not a spiritual defect. In some such way as this, by hasty generalization, he comes to believe in unlucky days and unlucky places. I do not think that there are any priests to teach him these beliefs, but, rather, that they are the result of careless observation, or faulty deduction from undoubted facts. Yet in attributing the belief in witchcraft chiefly to faulty observation and deduction, we must not overlook one element of truth in the asserted power of witchcraft, namely, the effect which mental states do, undoubtedly, exercise on the body. Emotion can increase or diminish nutrition, and profoundly alter secretions. A sudden shock may cause paralysis, insanity, or even death; and on the other hand, there seems little doubt, as Professor Maudsley argues, 'that the strong belief that a bodily disorder will be cured by some appliance, itself innocent of good or harm, may so affect, beneficially, the nutrition of the part as actually to effect a cure. . . . Ceremonies, charms, gestures, amulets, and the like, have in all ages, and among all nations been greatly esteemed and largely used in the treatment of disease; and it may be speciously presumed that they have derived their power, not from any contact with the supernatural, but, as Bacon observes, by strengthening and exalting the imagination of him who used them.'

It is this admixture of a little truth with much error, of a few facts with many fancies, which, no doubt, has gained for witchcraft so many adherents. Belief is infectious, at any rate the belief which is held by the large majority; and though it is difficult for any man to help yielding, for a time at least, to the current infatuations of his sect or party, he would probably soon cut himself adrift from any belief which had not some, indeed many, facts to support it. 'As to the imitative nature of credulity,' says Bagehot, 'there can be no doubt. In "Eothen" there is a capital description of how every sort of European resident in the East, even the shrewd merchant and the post-captain, with his bright, wakeful eyes, comes soon to believe in witchcraft, and to assure you, in confidence, that there "really is something in it." He has never seen anything convincing himself, but he has seen those who have seen those who have seen those who have seen. In fact, he has lived in an atmosphere of infectious belief, and he has inhaled it.'

The native feeling regarding a bewitched or unlucky place, is something like that of some Agnostic who replies when asked to live in a haunted house : 'No, I thank you ; I believe not in a spiritual world, but there are more things in heaven and earth than are dreamt of in our philosophy, and I do not care to bring myself into unnecessary contact with an apparently injurious and unknown force, whether psychological or otherwise.'

'No place is unlucky,' I said one day to a chief who objected to go to a certain village on account of its being unlucky, or fetish, or 'mwiko,' as he called it in the native language. 'Indeed,' he replied, 'then why did you leave the place you had been camping in and choose another?' 'Because it was unhealthy, and I should have fallen ill, and perhaps died, had I stayed there.' 'Yes,' he said, 'that is just what I mean; I shall get ill, and perhaps die if I go to that village. You call it unhealthy, I call it "mwiko," it is bewitched.' I was silenced.

There is nothing more in the belief in witchcraft than in the belief which many English people have in the unluckiness of spilling salt, of commencing any work on a Friday, of sitting down thirteen to dinner, or of walking under a ladder; nothing more in the practice of it than envy, spite and hatred, making use of the means which lie close to their hands.

I little thought beforehand what one effect of our strict observance of Sundays on the march would have on the observant natives. 'Do you know why we work as little as possible on Sunday?' I said to a small villager who was asking me many questions. 'Oh yes,' he promptly replied, 'it is your unlucky day.'

What is the case in West Africa, I am not competent to say; but in East and Central Africa I do not think the natives can, in any sense, be fairly accused of *worshipping* fetishes or charms, or the unlucky days, or other things which these charms are supposed to neutralize, any more than a somewhat superstitious Englishman could be fairly accused of being a *worshipper* of Fridays, or ladders, or patent medicines.

All believe in witchcraft; indeed, this seems the universal belief from north to south, and from sea to sea. No native in Africa ever dies a natural death according to the popular idea. If he is a man of any importance, an inquest is always held; a medicine-man casts lots, to see in whose hut lies the witch or wizard who has caused his death, and when the hut is discovered, the same unerring lot singles out the victim, who is thereupon tried and executed, the usual mode of executing being either to hack the victim to death with axes, or else to burn him alive. On one occasion a sub-chief at Mpwapwa went out hunting with a friend. Being, as most natives are, very careless with his gun, instead of shooting the game he expected to, he shot himself through his knee-joint, causing a bad compound fracture of the thigh. He died not many days afterwards, and an inquest was at once held to ascertain the cause of his death. The medicine-man called in discovered that he had been bewitched, and some poor innocent unfortunate was accordingly put to death.

This casting of lots is not all fair and above-board by any means. The medicine-man takes care that the lot does not fall at the door of a powerful man, or the probability is that the intended victim will make short work of him and his lots. Usually a friendless old man or woman is the unhappy victim ; this being the safest course, the medicine-man getting his fee, and the dead man leaving no one behind who will trouble to avenge him. But the medicine-man's lot is not all fees and feasting. He is credited with the power of bewitching people himself, and professional jealousy often incites a brother medico to rid himself of one who, as he considers, absorbs too large a share of his practice, the result being that the medicine-man makes his bed at last on the burning place to which he has consigned so many victims. Still the profession is always filled, though one would have thought that the pleasure of roasting even many other people would hardly compensate any man for having to undergo this agony himself. Another function of the medicine-man is to provide rain ; and great meetings are held at which monotonous musical incantations go on all day long, in the hope that rain may come. If it comes, he gets the credit of it, and if it does not come, he demands more presents, which he will hand over (when he asks him to do so) to the yet unpropitiated god. Sometimes, however, the disappointed people come to the conclusion that the medicine-man would make the most acceptable present, and he is accordingly offered up. Occasionally a person punished for witchcraft only meets the fate he richly deserves, as when a man who covets his neighbour's goods, threatens to bewitch him if he proves obstinate. I remember the case of an Arab, who, passing through a village up country, and being unable to obtain what he wanted from the people there, told them that he was going to bewitch them. They naturally came to the conclusion that it would be a very desirable thing if he died before his spells were completed, and accordingly they speared him.

The custom peculiar, in the civilized world, to the Jews prevails amongst certain tribes in the interior, whilst others never practise it. This rite is performed at about the fourteenth year upon boys, and in a modified form upon girls. The rite has apparently not been introduced by the Arabs, as many of the tribes who practise it hold little or no intercourse with them, and are far too conservative in their customs to follow the Arabs or anyone else. It appears to have no relation to any religious belief; indeed, there is practically no Mohammedanism in East Equatorial Africa, except on the coast and in the Arab settlements of the interior, which are few

A Jewish Rite 77

and far between. No one can say whence the rite arose, and why some tribes should practise it so carefully and some not at all. I have never even heard a theory suggested.

Most of the tribes seem devoid of much hair on the face, but not all, and those tribes which apparently have none at all have usually had some, which they have got rid of by artificial means; a hair is considered a blemish, and so the 'better dressed' men, if one may so term them, carry a pair of rough iron tweezers with them, with which they extract the offending growths.

Salutations differ amongst the different tribes. Most simply salute at a distance; but some shake hands, and this occurs amongst tribes who have never seen a white man, and who have little intercourse with the Arabs. I have seen a native who had just returned home from a distance meeting his friends, going up to them, placing his left hand on their shoulder and shaking the right hand with them, smiling away all the time, just as any warmhearted Englishman might do on meeting a very intimate friend after a long absence.

The style of huts built by the inland tribes has been described in a previous chapter; and from that it will be seen how isolated each hut is from its neighbour, an isolation which is increased by the self-supporting and self-contained character of each little community. Each tembé, containing four or five families, has its own farm or 'shamba,' upon which it raises millet seed, Indian corn, sweet potatoes, pumpkins, ground nuts, and usually some variety of bean, and a green vegetable. Both men and women work in the shamba, hoeing up the soil into high ridges, and planting the seeds on the top of the ridges just before the commencement of the heavy rains, and after the light rains have made the previously-baked ground soft enough to work. The ground is hoed up by means of a jembe, an implement like a large English hoe, with a spike behind, the spike being passed through a hole burnt in a long smoothed piece of wood, which serves as a handle. These hoes are made chiefly in Unyamwezi, where the natives have small charcoal furnaces and smelt the iron which is there found on the surface. They then become the chief article of barter, and are either used as hoes by the tribes who purchase them, or else forged into spearheads, arrowheads, billhooks, or axes. Each village usually has its forge for this purpose, the bellows being made of two cylinders cut from the trunk of a tree. the bottom of each cylinder is solid, and the top

AFRICAN SMITHY.

covered with a piece of goatskin firmly fastened round the edge, and with a rod fixed to the centre. The smith squats down between these cylinders and raises and depresses the rods alternately, the current of air escaping by a

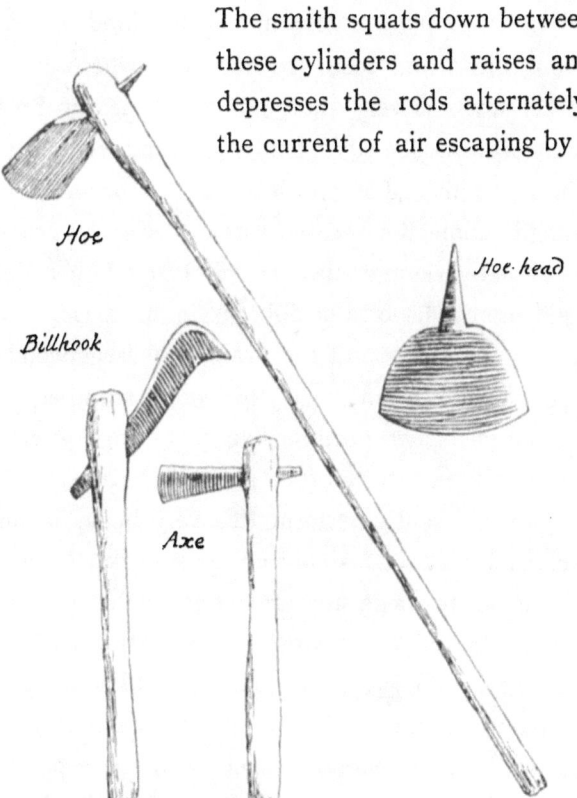

HOE AND OTHER IMPLEMENTS.

tube fitted into the lower part of each cylinder, the two tubes uniting together just in front of a small charcoal fire.

The grain raised on the shamba is gathered by women in harvest time, and brought home in baskets woven by women from the numberless kinds of long, strong grass and reed growing everywhere. The basket work is very thoroughly and neatly done; many of the baskets will hold water, and are by some tribes used instead of gourds for that purpose. When brought home the seed is stored in large tubs made of wickerwork and clay, which being larger than the doorways have to be built inside the house. The next step is to pound the grain in a large wooden mortar. Two women do this work together, the two large heavy pestles, five feet long, working alternately in one mortar in perfect time. The workers frequently perform this very heavy labour, each having a child fastened on to her back. They are careful not to waste any grain during this process; and to this end the mortar is frequently placed in a large, flat, shallow basket. This pounding takes off the outer husk, and the mixture is then winnowed very skilfully in shallow baskets, and the separated grain is finally ground to fine flour. This is effected by placing it upon a flat stone, and passing over this backwards and forwards a rounded stone with one flat surface. An incline to the large under stone gives the necessary inducement to the flour to collect in one direction. This grinding entails very hard work, much harder than that entailed by the two round horizontally-placed mill-stones which are used by the coast tribes, and which are so familiar to us in pictures of Eastern life. The flour so prepared is mixed with water and cooked into a thick porridge in an earthenware pot made out of a kind of iron claystone. This pot is supported on three stones for cooking purposes, and a wood fire lighted between them. The porridge or 'ugali,' as it is called by the natives, is the staple food of the interior. Millet seed ugali is much more sustaining than Indian corn, and the latter than rice. With their ugali the natives eat as a relish either dried half-cooked fowl, or beef or mutton treated in a similar way. When these delicacies are not to be obtained, ground nuts, pumpkins, or some other vegetables take their place. On the coast cocoa-nut is largely used as a relish with more satisfying food; but the cocoa-nut palm does not grow much, if at all, in the interior.

The soil is prepared for cultivation by burning down the trees, undergrowth and grass, and digging all the remains in. A farm is generally cultivated for two years, and then allowed to lie fallow for a year. The natives have no idea of alternation of crops upon the same soil, nor do they ever attempt to enrich it by using any of the manures obtainable; although land near a village is really valuable, as, so much being cultivated, if much lies fallow near the village it necessitates some of the residents having their farms perhaps two miles from home.

Each tembé keeps its own herd of cattle, sheep and goats, and its own fowls and occasionally pigeons. But the people pay little attention to the improvement of their cattle, making no attempt either to fatten them up, or to improve the breeds or keep them select. The only unusual product which I saw was a cow which was a cross between a buffalo and a domestic cow, but how it had been obtained I never ascertained. There are herds of donkeys far up in the interior, but again little attention seems to be paid to their breeding; they are very sluggish creatures. As zebras are so plentiful, I should think it would pay to cross the donkeys with them; such an experiment has been successfully tried in the Zoological Gardens, and the animals stuffed are now in the Natural History Museum at South Kensington. The animals are herded by the younger members of each family, who take them daily to the country round to find pasturage, and to the wells or streams for water. The cows supply the milk, which is usually drunk sour, or else kept for the purpose of making butter, which when rancid is used for anointing the body with, a more necessary custom than dwellers in temperate zones are apt to imagine. The naked skin needs protecting against the cool winds and night air of even a tropical climate, especially in the hills; and oil well rubbed in is as great a retainer of warmth as even a woollen vest. Natives, though not averse to washing, will never do so in any region where there are cold winds, unless they have a supply of oil at hand with which to anoint themselves afterwards. Many tribes rub on their skin a mixture of oil and clay to protect themselves not only against the cold, but also against the rays of the sun. For the same reason they also rub clay and oil on their calico when used as clothing, as it is not of sufficient substance without such treatment to protect them from either sun or wind. The chief at Mpwapwa one day received a present from a German settler of a handsome black Arab cloth gown, ornamented with silver braid. Next day he appeared in his new garment. It was almost unrecognisable; he had carefully rubbed in clay and oil over its entire surface.

When cattle are killed for food, the skins are scraped clean, pegged out on the ground hair downwards, and dried in the sun. The Waganda and some tribes in the south, amongst whom are the Bechuana, prepare their skins with great care, rubbing ingredients in to make them supple; but the less cultured peoples with whom we are concerned are content to simply clean and dry their skins. The skin so prepared is cut to shape with a knife, holes bored in it with an arrowhead, and thin thongs cut from it passed through these holes, and used to sew it into the required shape for use as clothing. On the caravan routes, fowls, eggs, and grain are bartered by the people for cloth, which, along these routes, is largely used for clothing instead of skins. By the same method of barter, old flint locks, and sometimes old muskets and ammunition, are obtained from passing caravans; but the spears, javelins, bows, and arrows are made by the natives themselves. Thus, with the exception of the iron hoe-heads, which are made by the Wanyamwezi, each tembé is quite independent, and able to provide itself with all the necessaries and, to an African's idea, all the comforts of life. Yet the African has little foresight, and will not store up to provide against failure in his crop; hence, even one scanty rainy season will cause a famine that will result in the death of large numbers of people, especially the very young and very old.

The African spends much of his time smoking under the shade of a clay and wickerwork awning. The pipe he uses is made from a gourd, and the smoke is inhaled through water contained in it, the water being changed as often as it becomes foul —foul, that is, to an African's taste. The tobacco grows in a little protected enclosure near his tembé,

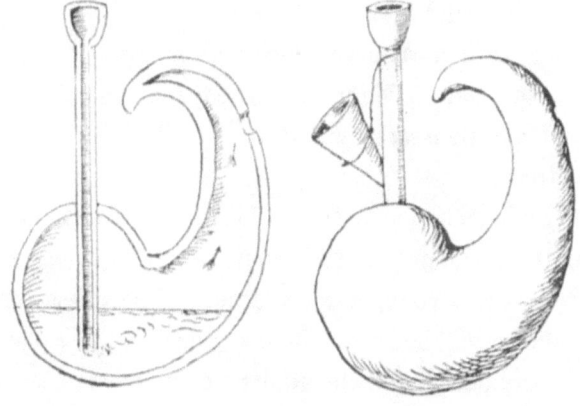
HOOKAH

and he dries it himself. We planted lettuces in our garden, and the natives mistook them when young for the tobacco-plant. I remember one year, when the tobacco crop was rather poor and behind-hand, that the natives came up to gaze in envy at the lettuces of a friend of mine, remarking: ' You *have* managed to get your tobacco well forward this year.' Indian hemp, or hasheesh, which I have nowhere seen growing, is also used by the natives in some districts. It produces a kind of intoxication, and the devotee to the hasheesh-pipe soon becomes a slave to the habit. Not only smoking, but snuff-taking is universally practised by the natives of both sexes. I remember a native who, seeing a European in bad health using some strong smelling-salts, went up to him, and asked to be allowed to try the white man's snuff, a request which was at once granted; and the native vigorously tried the white man's snuff, and then sat down on the ground in breathless amazement.

The boys and girls spend their time between herding the cattle or playing games, or idling, chiefly the latter. The younger ones amuse themselves with mimic spears, bows, and arrows, the elder ones play a kind of hockey, and the adults a game of marbles on a large board, the rules of which I did not succeed in ascertaining. In many places the 'ngoma' is a favourite occupation. Men and women stand round in a large circle, and one man and one woman from opposite sides advance towards the centre, dance a few steps round each other, sometimes holding hands, and then retire, to be followed by the next couple, and so on in endless succession, whilst a native drum keeps up a monotonous but not unpleasing succession of sounds, three or four in number, and varying in intensity, without intermission for many hours, sometimes even for a day and night. Lying about in the sun, or in the shade when that is too hot, seems to an African boy the summum bonum of existence. He does not naturally care for games, except such as require little exertion, and that little in extreme moderation. Probably it would not take many generations of *continuous* living in a tropical climate to reduce us to an approximately similar condition of chronic lethargy.

The East Equatorial African is not a warlike individual; he is timid and suspicious, and these characteristics often urge him on to acts of violence which he would not naturally commit. Of all the Bantu races in the district we are considering, the Mhehe, living in Uhehe, south of Ugogo, is the most warlike, and equalling him is the Masai, who, however, does not belong to the Bantu family. Yet the courage and ferocity of the Masai have been, I have no hesitation in saying, very much overrated by travellers, and I believe his reputation for bravery arises solely from the fact that he is less peaceable, and perhaps somewhat less timid, than the tribes by which he is surrounded. He has a wholesome dread of the white man, and is not likely to cause much trouble to the Imperial British East Africa Company, in whose sphere he chiefly lives. Indeed, he will probably be glad to come to terms with the company at the earliest opportunity, and may prove a very useful ally. I have seen some battles between different Bantu tribes, and the combatants frequently stand well out of range, and fire at each other with flint-lock muskets or other fossil weapons. Just before I went up into the interior, there had been a battle between two villages near the place to which I was going. They had fought for forty-eight hours, I was told, without a single casualty on either side.

The different tribes are very particular about the shape and ornamentation of their weapons, the spears especially; and the tribe to which men on the warpath belong can easily be recognised by the shape of the weapons they use. The small spear of the Mhehe, for instance, is very different from the small spear of the neighbouring tribes, but remarkably like the assegai of the Zulu, so much so, that when I showed some natives in the interior the coloured picture in the *Graphic* of the death of two officers in the Zulu War, they at once exclaimed, on seeing the weapons the Zulus carried: 'Why, those are Wahehe.' The accompanying illustrations of Kihehe, Ki Masai, and Kinyamwezi spears

Ornamentation of Weapons

will show the points of difference. A peculiar weapon, used apparently all over Africa, is one closely resembling the Irishman's knob-kerry, used for settling disputes in a friendly way. The knob-kerry, or 'rungu,' used by the Wa-Chagga at the base of Kilimanjaro is contrasted with that used by the Matabele, according to Mackenzie in his book, 'Ten Years North of the Orange River,' from which I have copied the engraving. It is used upon both men and animals, and when wielded by a skilful hand it is capable of inflicting an ugly wound upon a man. I have occasionally seen

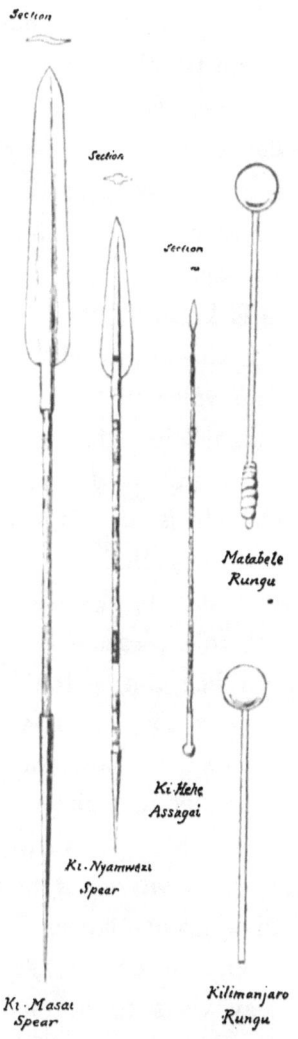

SPEARS AND KNOB-KERRIES

it used by the natives, but without any result, as it never hit the object at which it was aimed.

In many districts, the natives are obliged to wear anklets of roughly-made iron bells when they go out after dusk, in order to warn others of their approach, as a man approaching noiselessly at night is supposed to be bent upon mischief, and there is no penalty if he is killed. Under ordinary circumstances, if a man is killed by accident, the person who kills must pay his value to his relatives. Man being such a regular article of barter, there is never any difficulty in arriving at the damages to be paid.

The chiefs are chosen by the leading men. I rather think that in this selection the wealthiest men, as is natural, have most to say in the matter. Yet there is occasionally a man who is known as the chief's heir during the latter's lifetime; but I do not know how he is selected. The chief always seems to have more slaves and wealth of all kinds than any other man; this is natural, because each chief inherits the wealth of his predecessor, and adds his own riches to it. I have never seen a chief do manual labour, his principal functions being apparently to decide disputes between leading men, to pay visits to neighbouring chiefs, and receive visits from them. There are always sub-chiefs, but

Warriors

I do not know how they are chosen. The chiefs can call upon their men to fight, but rarely seem to organize them for war. The warriors do not appear to be ever drilled; but occasionally put on their war-paint and dress when going to visit neighbouring villages in a friendly way. Once I saw half a dozen in war-paint, shields and spears, indulging in a mock attack upon an imaginary enemy; when the enemy appeared somewhat unexpectedly in the shape of my mastiff and his puppy, who rushed up towards them, their curiosity excited at the sight of such strange creatures. But the warriors mistook the animals' innocent intentions, and made for the nearest hut, throwing away such impedimenta as shields and spears, in their headlong flight. We came up shortly afterwards, and explained matters to them, when they all came out again to obtain their discarded weapons, laughing heartily at their mistake, and evidently not in the least considering their conduct unwarlike.

When a chief dies, the fact is kept quiet until his successor is elected. If you happen to ask where he is, you will be told that he has gone to an adjacent district for his health. His successor, who is frequently his brother, is often not elected for some weeks; but when elected, he acquires at once all the property of his predecessor, including his wives; but his predecessor's favourite wife will not necessarily, indeed, not probably, be his; and if not, her bracelets and necklaces and other ornaments will all be taken off to grace the neck and limbs of his own favourite. I remember well two sable ladies, heavy with ornaments of brass and copper, who used to visit my wife, and sit upon the veranda whilst she talked or read to them, coming back after the death of the chief, their husband, dressed in dirty cloth, without a single ornament.

When girls become of a marriageable age, their parents have a grand feast, at which the fact is made public, and they can then be sought in marriage by any eligible young man. An eligible suitor is one who can give the parents the required number of cows. But a likely young man is allowed to pay a proportion of the cows at the marriage, and the rest afterwards. If the girl does not like her husband, she is by some tribes allowed to leave him, but her parents have to return the cows. Girls, however, are usually allowed some say in the marriage arrangements. I recollect being rather amused, one day, at hearing the reply of a pleasant-faced young woman, who was asked why she had refused the hand of the chief of the village;

(part of his hand, correctly speaking, as he already had two or three wives). She said he was too old, and too ugly. It was most true. A young man is not considered grown up until he marries; so a bachelor is not looked upon with very great reverence. I recollect when going, one day, to a strange village, a little chit of a boy marched up to me, stuck his arms out, put his hands into what would have been his pockets, had he worn clothes, and putting his head on one side, looked up at me, and said, in an impudent voice : ' Are you married ?'

On another occasion my wife and I had been visiting a chief of a small village, and as we were going away, we heard the steps of people running to catch us up; so we waited a moment, and up came two young men quite out of breath. As soon as he could get his breath, one of them said, pointing to my wife: ' How many cows could I get one like that for?' I tried to explain to him that in England people did not get their wives in that way. 'For nothing!' he exclaimed, delighted—' could I get one like that for nothing ?' I told him in answer to one of his questions that, if he came to England, he would be allowed to ask a woman to be his wife, but that I thought if he did so, she would probably say: 'No.' His friend, upon this, looked at him, and, bursting into a hearty fit of laughter said, with emphasis : ' Yes, I expect she *would* say, No.'

Both men and women, the latter especially, are very polite to white people, and they stand at the door when calling, and wait for an invitation before coming in. When on a journey down country on one occasion with my wife and child, the natives at most villages used to send a spokesman to ask us at what time it would be most convenient to us for them to come and see the baby, if we would allow them to do so.

I have spoken of the natural cowardice of many of the tribes, yet they are brave enough when with white men. When they know you, they trust you not to desert them, and so they will not desert you. Their cowardice is apparent more than real—as much caution as cowardice; a caution, too, the natural outcome of distrust, for untruthfulness is the curse of Africa, as it is of Eastern nations, and a native feels when fighting that he cannot place much confidence in his brother, and so acts as a man, who, though not particularly cowardly, is not particularly brave, often will act when he finds he has no one whom he can depend upon.

I once had to go to a village, near which a brother missionary lay ill, in order to warn him of an expected attack on the village by a hostile marauding band. I arrived at the village about midnight, and asked two of the men who were with me, and who were armed with breechloaders, if they would go up and give the alarm at the house, as I was tired with the walk. They were afraid to go, as the enemy, it was feared, might be lying in wait on the way; but they were willing enough to do so when I offered to accompany them, although I had no weapon of any kind with me. Wherever I have travelled, I have found it the same; if the native knows you, he will stand by you, and cheerfully go through dangers with you. I have found it the same even with the Zanzibari, unless, of course, the Arab comes into the question, under which circumstances, if he were to fight for you, he would be fighting against his own master, which you could hardly expect him to do; for the Zanzibari is the Arab's slave, even when he calls himself '*mngwana*' or 'free man.' But even under these circumstances he will not attack you himself. He will simply leave you undefended. At the time of the war between the Germans and Arabs on the East Coast, in 1888, Mr. Ashe from Uganda, and my wife with her baby and myself, were coming down country with a caravan composed largely of Zanzibaris; when the news reached us that the Arab Governor of the nearest coast town had ordered all white people and their native servants to be killed, and as we were the only white people near, he had sent up a well-armed convoy to destroy our caravan. The Zanzibaris came to us and told us the news; said that they were only slaves; that, therefore, though they would fight for our safety willingly enough against the interior natives, they could not fight against their own masters; but that they would not help them injure us, and would go to a village near, so as to be out of the way until, as they delicately put it, it was all over. Even, then, one of their number was found who, with an Mnyamwezi, willingly risked his life to take a message to the coast. So we wrote a tiny letter to the Consul-General, Colonel Euan-Smith, sewed it up in the seam of some calico they were wearing, took away their guns and other modern appliances, and gave them spears and bows and arrows, and disguised them as up-country natives. They travelled only by night, and in four days reached the coast town, where they were searched for letters, as all people from the interior were just then. However, they looked such savages that the search was not very careful, and they were allowed to go across to Zanzibar, when they at once took our letter to the Consul-General, who obtained from the Sultan a letter to the Arab Governor, ordering him to escort us down from our place of refuge, and making him responsible for our safety. Directly this order came up country, our Zanzibaris returned to us, and willingly helped us to get to the coast.

I was sorry to read in Professor Drummond's 'Tropical Africa' the following description of the Zanzibari:

'Here (Zanzibar) these black villains the porters, the necessity and the despair of travellers, the scum of old slave gangs, and the fugitives from justice from every tribe, congregate for hire. And if there is one thing on which African travellers are for once agreed, it is that for laziness, ugliness, stupidness, and wickedness these men are not to be matched on any continent in the world.'*

As regards the honesty of these porters, it fell to my lot in one period of a little over a year to arrange for the transit to or through Mpwapwa from the coast of over one thousand man-loads of goods. They were all brought up at intervals by Zanzibaris, and the head-man in charge was nearly always a Zanzibari. Yet when I came to check off the invoices and compare them with the goods, I found

* 'Tropical Africa,' p. 5.

all correct with the exception of one-third of a load of cloth, which had evidently been stolen by a Zanzibar porter, as he had dropped some of his dirty playing cards in while ransacking the bale. I have no great admiration for the morals of the Zanzibari; but I have known him for some years, and I must admit that he is, as a rule, surprisingly honest, kind-hearted, and faithful to his employer; and Captain Hore, who has known him about three times as long as I have, bears the same testimony to his worth. It is quite true that the native converts are better people to have on a mission station. What *should* we mean by conversion if they were not? And it is the case that the presence of Zanzibaris as workers at a mission station, with all their Arabian morals, is often a distinct disadvantage from a missionary's point of view. But though we may not desire them as co-workers in missionary effort, we have no right to deny their good and praiseworthy qualities, or libel them in such a wholesale way as is sometimes done, because they possibly tax the small stock of patience of an occasional traveller.

The native method of obtaining fire is ingenious, but only occasionally put into practice. A small log of dead wood is selected, and a hole half the size of the last joint of the little finger made in it. This log is now steadied by the native who seats himself on the ground for that purpose, and holds it with his feet; then taking a pointed stick, and inserting the point into the hole in the log, he rapidly twists it between his opened palms. The resulting friction first warms the wood, and then heats it to such an extent that it sets fire either to some tinder which he has previously placed round it, or, if the wood be dry, to the log itself. But this method is rarely required. In the villages fires are always kept burning, whilst on the march the camping-places frequently have fires smouldering. Occasionally at such places a fallen tree will be lit at one end, and left to smoulder. I have seen such a tree burning, and, repassing the same place four or five days later, have found it still alight. When the camping-place is in a village, the native usually takes a potsherd and obtains a fragment of live fuel from one of the huts; but even when all these things fail, he will light some tinder by the flint-lock of his gun, or by exploding a percussion cap, sooner than go to the trouble of obtaining fire by friction.

The Africans are a very musical race, and have many different kinds of instruments; but everywhere the same style of music. The commonest instrument is a kind of banjo made by fastening a large hollow gourd on to the wood of a bow tightly strung. The notes are produced by tapping the string with a slight wooden bar, and modified by pressing the open end of the gourd against the chest, or releasing it. Another less common instrument is like the toy which children at home play on, composed of a number of slips of glass fastened on two parallel pieces of string and struck by a light rod. In Africa pieces of very hard wood of graduated sizes take the place of the glass slips, and they are fastened on two parallel lines—the one made of a bar of wood, and the other of a piece of string or a strip of leather; another piece of hard wood forms the striker. The music generally consists of a few bars containing each two or three notes, of which the following is an example :

This is repeated over and over again, and sounds rather monotonous to European ears; but appears to have a peculiar exciting effect upon the native players, making them chant or play faster and faster until the climax is reached, and the time gradually slows down; but whether fast or slow, the time is always remarkably good. They evidently have a very clear idea of false notes, as frequently one player corrects the other for singing or playing a false note. A duet is sometimes played on the second instrument described, the hands of the performers constantly crossing during the performance of the piece; and it is amusing to see one, evidently the leader, scolding his companion for playing false notes or making mistakes which could only be discovered by the most educated ear, as it all sounds alike to the uninitiated listener. Sometimes the performers break out into song, and a third occasionally joins in upon a kind of flute, or rather flageolet, blown from the end like a penny whistle, which emits sounds absurdly like those produced by the highland bagpipes.

On the march the porters often sing to relieve the monotony of the way; and their chant, though most monotonous, has a certain soothing effect, which makes listening to it quite a pleasure. One, evidently the leader, begins with a sort of recitative, which he intones; and at the conclusion of this, two sets of men sing alternately as a chorus a two-syllabled word. For instance, one set sing:

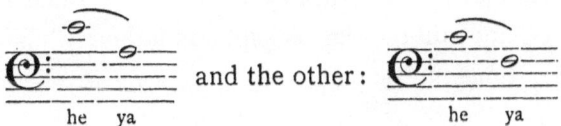

As they do so, they catch each other up in admirable time, though there may be twenty or thirty voices in each set, and separated some distance as they walk single file; sometimes pitching the notes high, sometimes low, with apparently no rule, though there evidently must be one, as there is nothing to jar even the most sensitive ear. At other times they will all sing in unison the following chorus:

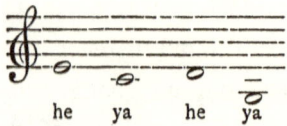
he   ya   he   ya

repeating it over and over again, sometimes for many minutes together.

It is difficult to describe the effect of this wild-sounding monotonous chant; but no one could hear it without being struck with the fascination there is to keep repeating it, and its soothing effect. The hammock-bearers, too, separated from the caravan, often keep up a song of their own as they carry the traveller at an easy trot. Frequently the song is only four words, repeated over and over again to two or three notes of music; but sometimes long descriptive pieces of poetry are set to the same few notes, and still the time is kept admirably; whilst at other times a comparatively short song is set to a much more elaborate piece of music, as in the following specimen :*

It is strange how well even the savage, uncultured natives understand the rules of chanting.

As regards the morals of the African native, I think the most striking feature, to a European, is his want of truthfulness. He apparently has no conception of the value or desirability of real truthfulness, and I suppose this feature he shares with most Eastern nations. Even amongst the Jews lying does not seem to have been definitely forbidden

---

* For this piece of Kinyamwezi music and the words (which are translated somewhat freely) I am indebted to the kindness of my friend, the Rev. W. E. Taylor, of the Church Missionary Society in East Africa.

in the decalogue, except where, as in the cases considered in the ninth commandment, it caused injury to a man's neighbours. You can only teach the African the meaning of truth by being scrupulously truthful yourself, especially in bargaining, a very large item of one's existence in the interior.

Of the sinfulness of drunkenness they also have no idea. Beer is only brewed two or, at most, three times a year as a rule, and on these occasions a whole village settles down to a steady drinking bout for two or three days, the drinking being accompanied by a monotonous chant, and equally monotonous incessant drumming, which never ceases day nor night, relays of drummers succeeding one another, until the bout is over, or everyone is hopelessly and incapably drunk. Once I had been reading through St. Luke with a native whom I was attending for a gunshot wound in the thigh. One day he informed me in an innocent way that he was going to get drunk on the morrow, evidently thinking that it would be a piece of information that would interest me, as I often inquired about native customs.

Near the coast a kind of wine called 'tembo' is made from cocoa-nut sap, and this is obtainable all the year round; hence drunkenness is far more prevalent at the coast than in the interior. To obtain this sap an incision is made into the stalk of a bunch of quite immature cocoa-nuts; beneath the incision a little bucket, usually made from a cocoa-nut shell, is secured and left there. The tree, at the

OBTAINING COCOA-NUT SAP.   YOUNG COCOA-NUT TREE

very summit of which is the fruit, has steps cut into it the whole way up; and by these steps the natives easily ascend to secure the cup full of sap, and replace it by an empty one.

In their outward behaviour before Europeans, the people are quite decent. In fact, a white man living amongst them will probably gauge their sinfulness in this direction to some extent by his own. If he is as careful of propriety in Central Africa as he would be in his own English home, he will probably find the natives extremely careful in their behaviour before him; and he may live amongst them for months, or years, without ever being offended by even an improper gesture on their part. Again, if he shows no pleasure in hearing descriptions of the unh'oly practices of the heathen, he will have none given to him. In this way he will fail to describe a part, and perhaps a not unimportant part, of the life of the Central African; but it is a loss not to be regretted. Can a man touch pitch, and not be himself defiled?

BANJO

CHAPTER IV

THE DAILY LIFE OF THE PEOPLE

THE daily life of the people can perhaps be best understood by a description of the events which occur during a day or two at some important village such as Mpwapwa. This village consists of a collection of about a hundred tembés, scattered over an area about two miles by one, each tembé sheltering three or four families, usually of people related to one another. On one occasion when I slept in such a tembé, I had to remain there until nearly mid-day, and so had the opportunity of observing all the consecutive occupations of the inmates.

At daybreak, which occurred about a quarter-past five, there was a stir amongst the sleeping forms, which up to this time had been wrapped in the light calico sheets which served as their garments in the daytime, and their bedclothes at night. They turned sleepily over, yawned, stretched themselves, and then gave a shiver; for the early morning, though warm enough to a man under blankets, was not very comforting to those whose only protection was one thickness of light calico. The women were, as usual, the first to rise, and got up, some from their resting-places on the ground, others from their simple native bedsteads, consisting of a light framework of wood, with an ox-hide stretched tightly across. The two or three yards of calico which had formed the wrap for the night was now re-arranged, and tucked round the waist as a sort of skirt. One of the children then brought a small gourd of water, which he carefully poured little by little over his mother's hands, who first washed her own hands and face, and then proceeded to perform the same office for her smaller children, an attention which they did not appear to appreciate. The next duty which fell upon the women and children was to sweep out the hut with brooms formed of one-foot lengths of ribbon-like grass tied together in bundles. They were most careful to sweep the hardened mud floor thoroughly, and this they did every day. If it were not for this, the place would soon have rapidly swarmed with vermin from the old animals in the courtyard, and from the calves, kids, lambs, and dogs, which slept inside the huts with the natives. I slept more than once in a hut, but was never troubled with vermin, so careful are the women to keep their floors well swept.

By the time the sweeping had commenced, the lords of creation had roused themselves; and after a similar re-arrangement of dress, and like ablutions, they refreshed themselves with a draught of water or some milk, and then helped the women fasten up the cows previous to their being milked, this duty being performed by the women. In Africa the cows will only yield their milk if they believe that the calf is abstracting it. So, in order to deceive the animal, the calf was allowed to commence operations, but after a few mouthfuls was tied up close to its mother's side, just out of reach of her udder, whilst one of the women, sitting down on a log of wood, placed an empty gourd in her lap, and rapidly milked the cow into it. When the supply of milk began to fail, the calf was again allowed to help itself to a few mouthfuls, which stimulated the mother into yielding a little more milk to the dusky milkmaid; but when this second stimulation had ceased to render any result, the calf was loosed, and allowed to extract what it could for its own benefit. A cow in East Equatorial Africa rarely yields much over three pints of milk a day, which is not surprising when one considers the scantiness of the herbage. The milk, besides being scanty, is occasionally tainted by the herbage on which the animal has fed, and often after it has fed on the rich rank grass in some marshy spot the milk is quite offensive. The gourds into which the milk was received were kept clean as far as natives could clean them; but rinsing with cold water will not remove the traces of sour milk from a wooden vessel, especially in a hot climate, and consequently milk received into these gourds becomes at once mixed with ferment from the old milk, and rapidly turns sour. This condition is not objected to by the natives, who either drink their milk sour, or else keep it until it is rancid, when they churn from it the butter which they use to anoint their bodies with. I have never seen this churning, but I believe that it is effected by shaking up the milk in a gourd.

When a calf dies, its mother refuses to give any more milk; but I believe that the skin of the calf, carefully dried, is used for deceiving her, and that if it is placed beside her at milking-time so that she can smell it, she will continue to give her milk for a long time after the animal's death. I have never had an opportunity of seeing this fraud practised.

Cooking Breakfast

The work of milking having been accomplished, the women commenced to cook the morning meal, which consisted of ugali (thick porridge) and uji (gruel), made from ground mtama (millet seed). When mtama is not obtainable, muhindi (Indian corn) is used instead; but it is not considered so satisfying, and consequently is not so highly valued as mtama. The men and women now sat in little groups round the fires over which their food had been cooked, and ate their morning's meal, which in the case of the children consisted of uji, whilst the men and women had ugali. The men, and some of the chief women also, took with their food some kind of relish (kitiweyo), such as a piece of dried meat, or some roast beans or pumpkins.

The food is not all 'dished up' in the same way; the more solid ugali is turned out into a wicker-work dish, or rough native earthen basin, and pieces are broken off and eaten by the men sitting round ; but the gruel-like uji remains in the pot in which it was cooked, and when it is sufficiently cool, the children, sitting round, each dip in their hands or a couple of fingers, and, withdrawing them, with great gusto lick off all the adhering uji. Hot gruel is very cleansing, and the hands, which are often very dirty before the meal, are usually remarkably clean after it.

It was now about eight o'clock, and the men strolled outside the hut or smoked a pipe inside; whilst the women nursed their infants, or, assisted by the children, washed up the few cooking pots. Not a long process, one would think; but all such domestic processes are long where there are no household conveniences in the shape of washtubs, towels, dusters, taps, sinks, and the like. Those who have gone on an expedition by river in England with a tent and a few requisites know the unexpectedly long time which it takes to get breakfast ready, and the still longer time which is spent in the apparently simple operation of washing up the dishes afterwards.

Towards nine o'clock the cattle were let out, and were taken by one or two of the elder boys to their usual pastures, and to water. As a general rule the elder boys are set to look after the cows, the younger ones after the goats and sheep. Until they are five the younger boys remain at home and play with each other; after that age, for a year or two, until they are old enough to take charge of the goats on the nearer pastures, they either follow their mothers and elder sisters down to the well for water, or else go with their brothers who are tending the herds, though they do not themselves give any assistance. These little mites often strike up great friendships with the smaller animals. I have often seen a little boy cuddling a lamb, or kneeling down with his arms round the neck of a calf, hugging and kissing it.

The natives are very particular not to let the cattle out before about nine in the morning, on account of the dew with which the long grass is saturated, and which is rarely all evaporated in the rainy season until the sun is half-way up in the heavens. Allowing cattle to wander about in the damp grass is a fruitful source of illness and death. The natives and Arabs know this, and are very careful; but strangers do not always know it, and occasionally suffer loss in consequence.

Soon after the herds had gone, the women, some with their babies slung on their backs, and the elder girls took their earthen waterpots and their calabashes and started off to fetch water from a three-foot well sunk in the river bed a mile away, laughing and chattering merrily as they went. An hour later they returned, and we saw them coming up the slope with their heavy burdens, freely perspiring in the tropical sun. Silently and slowly they toiled up the hill, reserving all conversation for another time when they would be a little less short of breath. As they passed beyond us, and we turned round to gaze at them, we saw far beyond them, on the plain away in the distance, what at first sight looked not unlike an enormous column of black ants in single file, but was, as we knew, a caravan some two miles in length, straggling along in detachments of forty or fifty men each. It was evidently bound for Mpwapwa, which the nearest men would probably reach in about an hour's time.

As soon as the women and girls had returned to the tembé and refreshed themselves with a short rest, they commenced the daily task of pounding corn and grinding it between two stones; slow, heavy, laborious work, which fully occupies them for an hour or two each day. Meanwhile some of the women went off to gather as firewood the dried-up branches of dead trees and bushes near by; whilst some of the slaves and younger men, axe in one hand, and spear or bow and arrows for protection in the other, went rather further into the forest than the women dared go, to cut off large boughs from the fallen trees in the less frequented places, far enough off to be not yet denuded of firewood. These men came back after three hours' absence, when the sun had been descending for two hours, and found on their return that there had been a great scare in the village. One or two men who had been herding their cattle a mile from the village on the very outskirts of the forest—too dangerous a place in which to trust boys with the care of these animals—had been heard to shout the war cry, and seen commencing to urge their cattle towards home at a gallop. Other herdsmen near took up the cry, and passed it on to yet others, until soon the whole village was in a state of excitement. The cause of this alarm was that the originator of the scare had assured himself that he had seen the zebra-hide-covered shield of a Mhehe lurking in the forest, and as no Mhehe was likely to be lurking alone thirty miles from his own village, there could be no reasonable doubt that he was but one of many others who had concealed themselves more carefully. The cattle being now out of danger, a small party of men, with ancient guns, proceeded to the point of danger. Seeing the commotion from the roof of my house two miles away, I ran down towards it with my boy, who carried for our protection a formidable looking double-barrelled breechloader, which, however, was quite useless, as the breech had got jammed so that it could not be loaded. But my boy did not mind that, as he felt sure no one would attack him with such a weapon in his possession. When we arrived at the scene of danger, rather out of breath with our long run, but hoping to be rewarded by the sight of a band of Wahehe in their picturesque war-paint, we discovered that the alarmist had truly enough seen the zebra skin as he described; but that it was still gracing the exterior of its original possessor, who had not yet been persuaded to part with his hide, and who had at once betaken himself into the depths of the forest at the sight of such an unusual commotion. After a hearty laugh all round at the man's expense, we returned to the village, and there found that the large caravan which we had seen in the distance had arrived; and that it had taken up its quarters down by the river bed, amongst the shade of the stately fig-sycamores. The leaders, we heard, were contemplating a prolonged stay of two days, for the purpose of drying their bales of calico, which had been soaked by the unexpectedly heavy rains of the previous few days. Two or three miles of this material lay on the bushes around, drying in the tropical sun, giving the camp the appearance of an enormous laundry establishment.

During the afternoon the porters from this caravan came up into the village to barter their goods for fowls and grain. For this purpose they brought with them cloth, wire, tobacco, and little supplies of gunpowder, perhaps half an ounce, wrapped up in dirty pieces of rag. With these they purchased the fowls and grain they required, pounded the latter in the mortar, lent by the seller, some of the more energetic also grinding it on his stones; but most of them were too lazy or too tired to perform this further labour, and took the grain back to camp there to boil and eat it whole. The mass so cooked, though it appeased the pangs of hunger, was of little use as food, and could hardly supply them with much staying power. Indeed, a walk through the camp, after the departure of the caravan, showed unmistakably that such food passes unaltered through the alimentary canal.

During the afternoon the elder men lolled in the shade, smoking pipes and listening to the news from the coast; whilst two also occupied themselves in unravelling calico, and then used the unravelled threads to sew the cloth together with, and another lazily ornamented a spear-handle with brass wire during the intervals of smoke and conversation. The children played or tended the herds, and the women continued their usual work of pounding, winnowing, and grinding corn, or else plaited baskets with dried reeds or grass. Apart from these, under the shade of another tembé close by, we noticed a young Mgogo carefully combing out and plaiting the locks of another man's hair. He used a comb with about a dozen large teeth, and having carefully combed one portion of his friend's rather matted shock of hair, plaited it up into rows of little pigtails, deftly weaving narrow bands of tough dried grass in each little tail, and finishing off by tying all together into one large tail, the end of which he neatly bound round with one or two dozen turns of the dried grass-bands. This hair-plaiting is such a complicated matter, and entails so much fine work, that a man cannot do it for himself, and so each native is dependent on his neighbour for his toilet. Even with the advantage which position gives them in working upon each other's heads, it takes two or three days to finish off one head in really correct style.

On my way to my house I met two Arabs, who were coming up from the camp, bringing with them a cheap Winchester repeating-rifle which would not work, and which they wished me to mend. This I was unable to do, or to give them a new key for the lock of a box, of which they had lost the proper one. They were much disappointed, as they had been counting for days on getting all put right, when

TEMBÉS IN UGOGO.

once they arrived at the station where the Englishman lived. Then they asked me to take charge of a load of cloth, which they were hoping the chief of the village would recover for them from a runaway porter, who had deserted a few miles from their present camp. This I willingly agreed to do, and a few days later the cloth was brought to me by the chief, who had caught the runaway in the meantime, and secured his spoil. This business transacted, I went down with them to the camp to see a sick Arab, who was suffering from an abscess in the foot, which had made the long daily marches almost unbearable to him. A timely incision with the lancet gave him immediate relief, to his great delight, and I told him to send up to the house for some dressings for his foot, for use on the march during the next few days. The dressing of a few ulcers and the extraction of a tooth completed my labours amongst them. They had but recently started from the coast, so that not many casualties were to be expected amongst them.

Later in the afternoon the women and elder girls again went down to the river-bed to fetch the supply of water for the night and early morning. Many of them went up the stream to a part where it was still running before it sank out of sight under its sandy bed, and there refreshed themselves by a bathe in its clear waters. On their return to the village they met the herds of cattle being driven home for the night; so, after they had put down their gourds of water, they tied up the cows and milked them again. With these women came a woman whom I employed to bring water daily for the house, but she carried a bucket on her head instead of a gourd, and prevented the water from splashing over by floating on it a few leaves and twigs. I should not have supposed this would have interfered with the motion of the water, but it did so most effectually.

The sun was now approaching the horizon, and shortly after six it set. The darkness then came on rapidly, though not by any means so instantaneously as one would imagine from some descriptions; yet a quarter of an hour after sunset the dusk was beginning to deepen, the herds were safe inside the tembé courtyards, and the fowls had retired into the tembés for the night, the natives began to gather near their tembés, the camp fires were lit in the caravan down by the river-bed, and for a few minutes an intense silence seemed to fall upon nature, broken only by the frequent call of guinea-fowl, quail, and smaller birds to each other, as they sought the safe retreat of the trees. It was a few minutes' silence only, and then the almost deafening din of myriads of insects broke upon the ear. The African insects seem to reserve their whole energy for the half hour of dusk, moderate quietness prevailing the rest of the twenty-four hours, except in the deeper forests, where the permanent dusk gives the insects the idea of perpetual sunset, and incites them to an unending low but piercing din. Darkness stole on apace, and by half-past six only a glimmer of light could be seen far down in the west. The camp fires now showed up well in the darkness, and also a fire a mile long on a distant hill, where the natives somewhat late in the season had been burning down the trees, bushes, and long grass to make a clearing for a farm. This fire had been burning all the afternoon, but only the smoke had been visible before in the glare of the tropical sun.

Inside the tembé the women now began to prepare the chief meal of the day, which consisted of ugali and meat—the men eating by themselves, and the women and children apart. After the meal, which was soon over, for they eat it quickly, notwithstanding the large amount which they managed to stow away, the men and elder boys sat round the log fire, and indulged in another smoke and talk over the events of the day, the prospects of the weather, and the likelihood of a neighbouring chief coming to make an attack upon them. There had been several raids of late, in some of which this chief's men had once or twice carried off a child or woman, and once had killed a woman at one of the outlying huts; though most of the raids had ended, as usual, in both parties shouting and violently threatening each other, and then retiring, feeling that the claims of justice and honour had been satisfied. There was, however, not much likelihood of more attacks being made that season. The time for cultivating had just commenced, and natives then (except such as the Masai, who do not cultivate, considering it to be menial work), have no leisure for marauding expeditions. They put off all such excitements until the more serious duties of the season are over. Nor do they fight during harvest, for to attack a neighbouring village at such a time would be to tempt the injured party to retaliate by coming over to burn the marauders' crops, and under these conditions both parties would have much to lose and little to gain. An African is a born bargainer, and carries his commercial principles with him into battle. War with him, in fact, is a species of trade, in which he endeavours to obtain by force and fraud what he has failed to get by fraud and hard bargaining. It is frequently conducted on strictly economical principles, and he realizes that the time to throw stones has not arrived whilst as yet he is living in a glass house. But the harvest safely gathered in, and all his grain and goods secure in his fortress-like tembé, he feels that he cannot do better than spend some of his spare time in the speculation of war. A chief who dabbles in this science has to carefully balance his accounts after each engagement. The value of a man is accurately known in cows; so many to a man (usually five), so many to a woman, so many to a child; and when the value of the booty has been summed up, from it has to be subtracted the value of the lives lost, and a balance on the wrong side soon deters a chief from continuing such engagements. It is this commercial instinct that makes the lives of the white man's mail-men so comparatively safe in Central Africa. They go often, only three in number, half across Africa; but they go well armed, and the natives on the regularly-traversed route soon discover that they carry only letters and books, which, to an African, is rubbish, if not worse (*i.e.*, witchcraft), and that attacking them means almost certain injury, if not death, to some of the attacking force, whilst there is nothing to be gained in the way of plunder as compensation.

By nine o'clock most of the natives had retired to rest, though a few men still remained up to talk over old times with an Mnyamwezi slave who had lived for a time in Mpwapwa some years back, and who was now passing by again for the first time since his departure, as he was on his way up country in the large caravan of the Arab which had just arrived.

But soon even these turned in, and now nothing disturbed the stillness of the night but the melancholy hooting of owls, the continual croaking of frogs rejoicing at the advent of the rainy season, the frequent harsh, grating chirp of the enormous grasshoppers, or the occasional howl of an hyena, or bark of an antelope or jackal.

The night passed as usual without any exciting occurrence, and next morning the daily routine commenced in the same way as on the previous one. But this was to be a more busy day, as the rains had softened the soil sufficiently to allow cultivating operations to commence; and the first attempt would be made to hoe the ground previously prepared by destruction of the undergrowth. There was also another excitement in the day's programme; before the herd were led away to the grazing-grounds, a very lean cow, past the period of calf-bearing, was selected for the butcher's knife, as the presence of such a large caravan, staying as we have seen for two days, would make it worth while to slay a useless cow, as there would certainly be a great demand for fresh meat. The cow was led apart from the herd, and a native warrior, anxious for some gun practice, took his stand near the animal at the distance of only a few paces, and taking a long and patient aim fired at its body, which he succeeded in hitting. The shot, however, did not appear to do any immediate damage beyond making the animal jump, which so disturbed the aim of a second warrior, who was preparing to send another charge into it, that he fired somewhat at random and accidentally sent a bullet through its heart. The cow fell at once, and another warrior, armed with a cheap butcher's knife made of soft iron, probably in Birmingham, now seized its head and deftly cut its throat from ear to ear. After all bleeding had ceased, the animal was skinned, disembowelled, and hacked to pieces with knives and blunt hatchets. An hour later, after much shouting, bargaining, wrangling, laughing and joking, the whole animal had been disposed of, and the owner sat down to count his gains—calico, coloured cloths, gunpowder, percussion caps, tobacco, beads, wire, cheap knives of soft iron, and hoes, forming the chief articles of barter which he had acquired.

The usual early morning's work finished, several of the women, and some of the men of low degree, went off to the tract of land about a mile away from the tembé, which the owner had lately marked out for cultivation, and had cleared of undergrowth and grass by burning. Amongst the East African tribes a man's title to land seems to be acquired in the same way that it is in civilized countries. The forest and waste lands which lie between the villages belong to no one; anyone may clear and till as many acres as he chooses to, and whatever he tills becomes his property. If he sows it one year, he will probably let it lie fallow the next, but it still remains his until it has become completely overgrown again with trees—not with brushwood merely, for in such a hot climate brushwood springs up again in a very few months after the rains. At his death his cultivated land, together with his other property, huts, treasures, wives, children, all goes to his heir, who is usually his eldest surviving brother. In this way the land in the villages, as well as that on the outskirts, was no doubt originally obtained, and now passes on from heir to heir. When I wanted land near the village, I went to the chief, who asked me for what I required it, and it was given to me at the rate of about sixpence an acre; but I think that the chief's permission is asked by each native before he tills near the village, not so much because the chief owns the land, as because he owns the man who wants to till it, and who must just as much obtain his leave before he pays a visit to a neighbouring village as before he takes twenty acres of land from the forest.

But to return to our labourers who had just arrived at the clearing. They at once set to work, and continued for two or three hours hoeing the ground up into ridges about eighteen inches high, and in this way well broke up the ground for twelve inches below the surface. Some days later, when the whole clearing had been well hoed, the same people would walk alongside each ridge, make holes with a stick at intervals of a few inches, carefully drop one or two seeds into each, and then cover them over with soil. There is no wasting of seed here, no sowing on the roadside, or in shallow rocky ground. Later on, when the young corn began to sprout, women would walk along each furrow, and great pains would be taken to root up every weed that endeavoured to put in an appearance; and at last when the corn was ripening into heads of grain, small boys would be sent to watch the fields all day long, and frighten off every bird that tried to approach; no easy task in a land where there are such immense flocks of very small birds as there are in Africa.

Whilst these people were cultivating the farm, or shamba, as it is called, two natives were engaged in the village in burning charcoal. They selected very hard close-grained wood, which they cut into blocks, stacked, and then burnt under a covering of clay. The resulting charcoal in small pieces was placed in a basket and set aside for use next day at the forge, for there was one tembé which possessed a small forge, and had inmates who could work it.

Some distance off we noticed a few men who were building a new tembé, not far from their old one. They used chiefly new wood for the purpose, but also drew largely upon the old tembé for such timbers as had not been destroyed by the rains or the ravages of the white ants. Tembés rarely last much over ten years, even with frequent patching; as the white ants destroy most of the timbers by that time, and even where they do not, a tembé has often to be evacuated on account of what, for euphony's sake, we might call 'the drains going wrong.' The natives bury their relatives inside the tembés, and usually not very deeply under the floor, and too many relatives so close underneath is apt to make even a native feel the desirability of change of air. It looked at first sight as if the men were doing the work, and the women tendering a little assistance; but we noticed on closer inspection that though the men were standing in a conspicuous place on a portion of the newly-made flat roof, arranging the stones and clay on it, the women were bringing the heavy loads of stone and clay from a distance and lifting them on to the roof. It was quite in keeping with what is considered woman's work in Africa. Our mistake reminded me of the story of the young Irishman who was delighted at being engaged as a hodman. 'You will have no work to do,' said the sympathetic contractor; 'you have only got to carry bricks up a ladder, and the man at the top does all the work.'

Towards mid-day we heard a great deal of shouting at the foot of the hill, and were told that some native hunters returning from a week's chase were rejoicing with their friends over their spoil. They had killed an elephant with their poisoned arrows, and had brought back in addition to the ivory a good supply of elephant meat. This appeared to consist of the skin and flesh cut into long strips about three inches wide and two thick, somewhat resembling leather straps, and not altogether unlike them in flavour and consistency, whilst three days exposure to the sun and flies had not improved their odour. I bought two strips for my dogs to eat. They were greatly pleased at first, and set to with a will, but after fifteen minutes' hard work they had reluctantly to admit that they had attempted a task beyond their powers, and that elephant meat baffled even a mastiff's jaws.

Whilst the meat was being disposed of, a caravan of about two hundred porters from the far interior, consisting chiefly of slaves, began to approach the village and to form their camp near that of the large caravan which had arrived on the previous day. The greater part of the loads was made up of tusks, some of eighty or even ninety pounds weight; far too heavy for one man to carry, but carried, nevertheless, by some of the more powerful slaves. Many of the smaller tusks weighing from ten to thirty pounds each were tied into bundles of three, and each bundle carried as one burden. Besides ivory there was quite an assortment of miscellaneous articles, which the owners were only too ready to barter to a white man. One brought me a baby ostrich, about the size of a turkey, which he wanted me to buy for fifteen rupees; and another brought me a talking parrot from Manyuema on the Upper Congo, the country of Tipoo Tib, for which he suggested I should give him forty rupees. I did, in the end, purchase some cloth made from the bark of trees which came from Uganda, and a baby gazelle, looking like a rat on stilts, which the boys and I fed most carefully with milk and water from a baby's feeding bottle : a process, however, which it did not long survive, though it took very kindly to it at first.

Early in the afternoon the women and slaves returned from the shamba which they had been cultivating, and recommenced their miscellaneous occupations. One man made holes with a hot iron in some axe-handles, which he had roughly carved out of a piece of wood the week before. He worked at each hole and kept trimming and enlarging it until the long narrow wedge-shaped axe-head could pass one-third of its length through and then be gripped. This is the only fastening which the axe-head has, and consequently it not infrequently comes out during use; but then it is quite easily replaced. Another man was cutting little stools out of the trunk of a fallen tree which happened to be of the required diameter. The tree selected for this purpose is always one with hard wood, frequently the ebony tree, and the little three-legged stool, with a disc above and below, is cut out in one piece, and then trimmed with a hot iron and a knife—a long process, and one which would be very tiring if it were not that the artist took plenty of time over it; as, indeed, a native does over every kind of work. The number of hours which a native works is very little criterion of the amount of labour which he performs.

Although, as on the day we are describing, we frequently see different people doing different duties, there is very little real division of labour. All the people turn their hands to everything, and the difference between the individual workers consists in the fact that some seem incapable of performing some duties, and consequently relegate them to all the others, rather than that any are considered adepts at any particular kind of work. It is as if, in England, everyone should paint pictures for sale and sing in concerts, except those very few people who were either colour blind, or deaf to the difference between harmony and discord.

There was a good deal of excitement in the village this afternoon, owing to the discovery that six of the chief's donkeys, which he had lost a week previously, were in the caravan that had just come from the interior; the Arab leader of which asserted that he had bought them from a caravan passing westward, which he had met a few days back. There was little doubt that they had been stolen by the leader of this westward-going caravan, and sold by him to the Arab in charge of the other, who would be able to buy them for a trifle, knowing that he had to run the risk of getting them safely through Mpwapwa. After a great deal of altercation between the chief and the Arab, and after solemn protestations by the latter that he had purchased them in the innocence of his heart, and assurances that he could not possibly afford to give up animals, such wretched animals, too, for which, being in great need of them, he had had to pay such a high price, they finally agreed to share losses, and each to take half the donkeys. This matter settled, the Arab asked me if I would come down to the camp with him, and see some of his sick people. On the way we passed two Wagogo in full war dress and paint. They looked very proud of themselves, and told me that they were going away for a few days to a Masai village some fifty miles off, to see some friends of theirs. They could speak the Masai language, a rare accomplishment amongst the Wagogo; as the languages are not at all akin, as we have seen. A little further on a couple of boys brought me a small kingfisher, which one of them had shot with an arrow, blunted at the end so as not to injure the plumage; for which they asked me to give them some sweetmeats. I told them to bring me the bird when I went home again; so they wandered off quite happily, with their arms round each other's waists. The boys and young men often go about in couples like this, and really seem very much attached to one another. There seems to be more affection between men and men, and between women and women, than between the sexes.

As I was passing my milkman's hut, I stopped to have a talk with him, as I wanted to purchase milk from him by the fortnight, instead of, as usual, by the month, or rather, moon; but I could not get him to see that one doti (four yards) of calico every fortnight was as good pay, in fact rather better, than two dotis a month. The man refused to let me have the milk on these terms; so I was obliged to give in, and let him supply it on his own terms. I found the same difficulty in explaining to natives who did daily work, that an upande (two yards) of calico every two days, was the same pay as twelve upandes a month of twenty-four working days.

The natives everywhere seem to have very rudimentary ideas of arithmetic; and the few calculations that they do, they usually work out upon their fingers, as would be done by a little child in England.

When we arrived at the camp, we found that there was an altercation going on between an Mgogo sub-chief and some Zanzibaris. The latter, members of the caravan that I had come to visit, were lighting their camp-fires as usual at the foot of a splendid fig-sycamore. These trees, not many in number, only grew along the moist stream valley; and were being gradually destroyed by the camp-fires which were so frequently lit first at the base, and then in the hollow which previous fires had excavated. Of course such a hollow made a capital fireplace, sheltered from gusts of wind, whilst the over-hanging well-foliaged branches of the great tree protected the whole camp from the sun in the day-time and the dew or rain at night.

After examining all the sick people, it was evident that two of them were too ill to travel; and the Arab asked me to take care of them until his return from the interior, which I agreed to do for a shilling a week, the actual cost of their food. The unfortunate creatures were suffering from dysentery, and were so extremely emaciated, that one died a few days after he came to me; but rest, warmth, good food, and medicine pulled the other through.

On my return to the house, my boy told me that the natives at a tembé close by wanted me to lend them a steel-trap, as a leopard had just come down from the hill; and in broad daylight, a most unusual time for such an attack, had attempted to carry off a goat which had wandered a little apart from the flock. The little boys who were tending the goats had bravely rushed at the animal with their spears; and he had at once dropped his victim, leaving it dead on the ground, and retreated up the hill under cover of the brushwood. The natives knew that he would return at dusk to look for his prey, and they were anxious to trap him when he did so. My boy took the trap over to the place; and having securely lashed the body of the goat to the stumps of two trees, tied the trap firmly over it.

Towards sunset, an Mgogo sub-chief came up to the house with his wife, as she was suffering from an inflamed ear, which he wished me to treat. She was a very light-skinned woman, hardly darker than some Italians, and her husband was very fond of her. The higher classes of natives seemed often to be fond of their wives, and also of their children.

Discipline for the Young

They would carry the latter long distances to get them attended to at the dispensary, and they looked after them very tenderly when they were ill.

Whilst I was attending to the woman's ear, we heard violent screams from the tembé nearest to us; and my boy told me that the owner of it was chastising one of his children for having run away to play that afternoon, whereas, as he well knew, it was his turn to herd the goats. Though both fathers and mothers are fond of their children, yet they fully agree with Solomon, that sparing the rod is likely to spoil the child; and they do not wish to spoil him.

Although relations are attached to one another, and ties of relationship are binding, yet the effect of this is much diminished by the large number of artificial relationships which are observed, and which almost swamp the real ones. A man considers every other male member of his tribe to be his brother, and gives him the same title as the child of his own father and mother. Again, a man addresses and speaks of as 'mother' the woman who cooks his food for him, if he happen to be a bachelor; so that when a man travels much and lives in various villages the number of his close relations becomes apparently very large. I was very much struck with this in the case of my boy, when first I went out to Africa. Soon after he came to me he asked leave for a day's holiday, as his mother, he told me, had died, and he wished to bury her. I was very sorry for him, and at once gave him leave to go. A month later he wanted another holiday, and his mother died again.

After tea my boy and I went over to a tembé near by to take some soup, thickened with rice, to an old man suffering from dysentery. We found him lying down, wrapped up in a blanket which we had lent him, and for which he was very grateful. He said that the cold wind at night no longer caused him the pain inside which he had suffered from before, and that now he slept all the night through. He only drank boiled water, which he obtained from a little kettle we had lent him. I had insisted on this, because water at this season (the commencement of the rains) was especially filthy; and though only occasionally harmful to a native in good health, would be very dangerous to one already suffering from dysentery. After a time this old man got perfectly well, contrary to the expectation of all his friends; and he became a great help to me in persuading others, when they were ill, to carefully follow out my instructions as to rest and warmth and diet, which he assured them were more important than even medicine. Whilst I was examining him, we noticed a strong, rather unpleasant smell of meat in the tembé, and asked what it was caused by. He told us that they were drying some of the meat from the cow which had been killed that morning, and showed us the joints and strips of flesh hanging from the roof timbers over the part where the fires were lit, and where the women were cooking the evening meal. This meat was being dried in the usual way previous to being stored away for future use. Suddenly we were all startled by the sound of loud deep growls and horrible snarling breaking the silence of the night, coming from a hollow in the hill-side close by, and then we remembered that it was the spot where we had fastened the trap on the body of the goat. Evidently the leopard was caught, so off rushed the natives and my boy with spears and guns; but the night was dark, and no one was anxious to walk unexpectedly within reach of the leopard's paw, so they approached very cautiously, stood some yards from the dim snarling figure, and commenced to fire at it. But what with the unusual darkness, and the usual bad shooting, they fired fifteen shots at him before he was killed. Next morning when I came to examine the trap, I found that a piece of scrap iron which one of the natives had fired out of his gun, had made a hole right through the strong iron plate which was between the jaws of the trap.

After half an hour's absence they all came back to the tembé, bearing with them in triumph the dead leopard and the slaughtered goat. There was a great deal of rejoicing at the destruction of this enemy of the peace, and the rejoicing was considerably augmented by the prospect of a good feast off the carcase of the goat, which they at once commenced to cook. Whilst the meat was being cooked, and after the excitement of the party had somewhat cooled down, a young man played a monotonous, but not unpleasing air on the native banjo.

On the way home I nearly shot one of my mastiffs. He had been walking behind me, and I thought he was still doing so, when, having wandered off through the long grass, he suddenly jumped over a bush on to the path right in front of me. In an instant my gun went up to my shoulder under the impression that it was a lioness; but happily I discovered my mistake before it was too late. I realized then what kind of feeling it was that so frequently made the natives rush into their huts, or make a bolt up the trees when I went unexpectedly into a village with my dogs.

After reaching home I went the round of my patients to see that they were comfortable; and this duty finished, had prayers with the boys, after which we were all glad to turn in for the night.

CHAPTER V

THE CLIMATE AND DISEASES

An Englishman need have no difficulty in realizing for himself the climate of Africa. He has only to imagine the time from mid-day to early afternoon, on the hottest day of an unusually hot English summer, and he will understand what Eastern Equatorial Africa is like from eight in the morning to half-past four in the afternoon of the greater number of days in the year. A heavy thunderstorm on such a day, with its attendant cooling of the air, and hiding of the sun, will give him an equally true idea of the rainy season. The first thing that usually strikes an Englishman on arriving, is that the heat is not nearly so great as he had pictured to himself. In fact, if he arrived in the dry season he would very likely revel in the glorious golden sunshine of an endless August; he would enjoy the genial warmth, and wonder why the older residents were so careful to avoid the sun, and were so far less energetic than himself. But as months went by he would change his opinion. The unending summer's day soon palls by repetition. The man who delights in it is perhaps seized by some attack of illness. He lies perspiring on his convalescent couch, and longs for a cool wind; in vain he tries to shield his now weakened eyes from the splendid brilliant sunshine that he once so much enjoyed. He hopes for a cool season, for some weather to brace him up, but hopes in vain, and he begins to realize, as he never did before, the inestimable blessing of a European winter. This is the first step towards so-called acclimatisation. He has gone a few steps down the ladder of health. Soon he will reach the highest level at which it is possible for the average individual to keep in East Africa. He will cease to take quite such an interest in his work; his head will ache more easily; his digestion get impaired with less reason than formerly; he will get more quickly tired after exertion of any kind. The enervating climate has done its work, and in the course of a year or two he finds himself on the level described. Later illnesses do not pull him down so much proportionately as the earlier ones did; the conditions before and after attacks are less far removed than they used to be, though attacks are more prolonged;

a sore throat acquired is not easily lost; a scratch which ought to heal in a few days becomes an indolent, not very troublesome, but continuing ulcer. In brief he is acclimatised, grand result! One hears much of acclimatisation in tropical countries. I cannot speak of the condition elsewhere than in East Equatorial Africa; but there, at any rate, I do not believe there is such a condition in the ordinary sense of the term. The man best suited to withstand the climate is the *healthy* man fresh out from England or elsewhere, with all his English strength and vigour. The next best man is the resident who has just returned from getting in a fresh stock of health and vigour in some temperate climate. One thing that tends to keep up the mistaken idea that there is such a thing as acclimatisation, is the obvious fact that the man who has been out longest, cæteris paribus, knows best what precautions to take, and as a rule takes them, and so escapes disease which the new-comer unnecessarily lays himself open to. For the same reason, at home, the confirmed dyspeptic often lives longer than the ordinary man. He takes far greater care of himself than another man, as he knows the pain which he will suffer if he commits indiscretion, which another man may indulge in with apparent impunity, for many years at least. Yet no one would think of calling the dyspeptic a man 'acclimatised to the ills of life,' or desire the same acclimatisation for himself.

Throughout East Equatorial Africa there are two distinct rainy seasons—the lesser and the greater rains—which occur at different months at different distances from the coast. At the coast the lesser rains begin the middle of October or early in November, and last for a month or six weeks. The greater rains begin the middle of March, and last about two months. The hottest season is during the two months preceding the greater rains. Near Victoria Nyanza and Tanganyika the lesser rains do not commence until towards the end of December, and the greater rains are proportionately later. In the intervening country, the date of the seasons approximates to that of the coast or lakes according as the district is nearer the one point or the other. In the mountain districts also these same seasons occur; but in addition there are frequent showers, and in parts thunderstorms also, all through what in the adjacent plains would be the dry season. The climate of the high upland region between Kenia and Kilimanjaro I am not acquainted with; but it ought to be comfortably cool, and the district well watered, judging from the corresponding district further south, where the elevation is not nearly so great.

The climatic diseases that Europeans going to Central Africa must be prepared to meet are chiefly sunstroke, malarial fever, dysentery, and typhoid. But the severe form of malarial fever is, except in isolated spots, confined chiefly to the coast-swamp and the first plateau—the one absent, and the other not extensive in the British region; whilst dysentery is, I believe, caused entirely, and typhoid chiefly, by drinking impure water, which with proper care need never be done.

Under the name 'malarial fever' are usually described (1) fevers caused by the poisonous atmosphere of swamp regions; (2) those caused by drinking impure water which rises in and passes through such regions; (3) those caused by exposure to the sun; and, lastly (4), typhoid fever. The severe form of malarial fever, due to contamination of the air, is confined chiefly to the two regions described above; but also exists where there are marshes or low-lying swampy districts even as high as the central plateau. Dr. Felkin gives four thousand feet as the height above which malarial fever is not found. This, though in the main correct, is mis-

Impure Water

leading. The severe form even is found above that elevation in low-lying districts, especially in hollows amongst the hills, as where a comparatively large valley has a very small, not steep, outlet. Such basins as these are imitated on a small scale amongst, for instance, the mountains in the lake region of England; and travellers who have left the beaten tracks and clambered over the hills find the same grassy swampy hollows amongst the slopes. The comparatively severe cold of the higher regions will, even where there is no malaria, bring out any fever latent in the system, just as an English winter will do in one lately returned from Africa; so that a visit to a hill-sanatorium is sometimes disappointing to an invalid who hopes for a speedy, as well as thorough, recovery.

Drinking unboiled water, however clear-looking, is a *very* dangerous proceeding. Even in the healthy upland districts such an indulgence is apt to cause, amongst other disasters, the severe form of malarial fever; but whilst impure water is one of the sources of malarial fever, it is the chief, if not only, source of dysentery, and the chief source of typhoid. This is not to be wondered at, considering the unsanitary habits of the natives, who turn all their streams into sewers. The traveller has only to walk a short distance along a path by the side of any stream to see at a glance the cause of the streams being fouled. Even the cleanest-looking, fastest-running streams are somewhat dangerous on this account, and the smaller or semi-stagnant ones highly so. Before I went abroad, Commander Cameron, the African traveller, advised me to drink unboiled water from the running streams only; but the difficulty in following out such advice as this lies in the fact that a traveller does not go to the stream to fetch his own water—his boy goes for him; and unfortunately an African boy's idea of a running stream is a stream that runs sometimes. I would therefore unhesitatingly advise that a man should never drink unboiled water in East Africa, except where he has a spring in or close to his own garden. If he follows out this precaution, and does not sleep in swampy districts, nor expose himself unprotected to the sun, he will, in all probability, never have a *severe* attack of fever; he will certainly not get dysentery or sunstroke, and he will almost certainly not get typhoid. In fact, East Africa, except in parts, is not dangerous to the traveller who will let the habit of taking precautions become a second nature to him. Taking precautions may be a trouble at first, but in time it will cease to be so, and the traveller or resident will be no more conscious of trouble when taking precautions than he is when taking the necessary steps to wash and dress himself each day.

The streams are always in their most dangerous state at the beginning of the rainy season, when the showers first moisten the refuse lying about, and thus cause its decomposition, and then wash the decomposing materials into the nearest stream. At this time dysentery, typhoid, and diarrhœa are very prevalent amongst the natives, and frequently attack the white man who is imprudent enough to drink the water direct from the streams.

Natives are not constitutionally exempt from many, if indeed from any, of the diseases from which Europeans suffer; but being uncivilized, they escape many of the ills which civilization brings in its train, whilst they also fail to profit by the protection against other evils which civilization provides. There is no wine or ardent liquor, and little fermented drink in the interior, consequently there are none of the many ills that result from over-indulgence in these beverages. There is, of course, no painter's colic or knife-grinder's phthisis. There are, it is true, no boots to cause corns on the upper surface of the feet; but the rough, rocky paths frequently cause corns, fissures, and ulcers on the soles of the feet, very painful and very intractable. Natives do not suffer from sewer-gas poisoning, but they suffer to an enormous extent from permitting the same refuse to poison their streams. There is no short-sight amongst them; but dirt, and the glare of the sun and the dust-laden winds, cause frequent ophthalmia, which being neglected produces the various degrees of blindness so prevalent in these regions. Though they have not yet learnt what nervous attacks, as we call them, mean, they are not free from St. Vitus' dance, epilepsy, and madness; whilst stammering is about as common a complaint as it is in England. I do not recollect having seen a case of spinal curvature, nor would one expect to find it amongst people who are unclothed and wander about much in the open air. Hare-lip and cleft-palate has its victims in Africa as much as in England.

Leprosy (anæsthetic and tubercular) is not uncommon amongst the races of the interior; and as there are practically no streams (except near the coast) in East Equatorial Africa, it is hard to see how in these districts it can be produced by fish-eating, as a very eminent authority believes is usually the case. The only fish ever seen in these regions is

Leprosy

dried shark, carried up into the interior, as everything else is, on men's heads, and therefore an expensive article of diet, used only as a relish, and even as that, its use confined to the porters who come up in the caravans, whilst leprosy is found amongst the residents in the interior who have never been to the coast.

Small-pox is endemic in Africa, and most caravans have a case amongst them. The natives are well aware of the infectious nature of the disease, and frequently burn down the temporary huts left by each passing caravan in order to destroy any possible contagion of this virulent and dreaded disease. Some of the tribes practise inoculation amongst themselves, and are eager to be vaccinated when they have the opportunity, frequently coming long distances to a mission station for that purpose. Although small-pox is endemic, perhaps because it is so, the natives do not suffer so severely from the attacks as white people do. A severe form of the disease, in which the eruption is of the character known as 'confluent,' and which is very fatal in Europe, is usually recovered from by them; and frequently they never even feel ill enough to stay on their beds even for one day during the attack.

From the accurate descriptions by Ashe and Mackay, it is evident that the plague does rage in Uganda, notwithstanding what authorities state to the contrary; but I have never come across the disease in the more southerly regions. I have never, either, succeeded in recognising measles or scarlatina, though I am not at all sure that they are not to be seen. Isolated cases of what is apparently a not very rapid form of cholera I have come across; the disease causing death, when it does cause it, in from two to three days. Epidemics of cholera I have never seen or ever heard of as occurring in the interior. In fact, the epidemics that I have seen have always been of a mixed type of disease, and in almost every case easily traceable to bad drinking water; a small collection of people being all, perhaps, taken ill on the same day, some with malarial fever, some with dysentery, some with typhoid, some with dengue, and some with diseases to which I could put no name. Certainly life in Central Africa inclines one to the belief that filth does cause so-called specific diseases to be generated de novo, and that hybrid diseases are far from uncommon; but to satisfy oneself on such a point as this, would require a far longer stay in the interior, and far more extended experience than I have had.

I would strongly advise anyone interested in the study of disease, and intending to travel in Central Africa, to read, first of all, a small monograph by Dr. Collins on the above question.*

Umbilical hernia is extremely common in children; but rare in men, evidently disappearing as they grow older. This tendency is increased by the children's diet, which consists of large quantities of grain food, and some vegetables, with little, if any meat; a diet which produces a degree of distension of the abdomen very strange to the European eye. The same grain-eating habits in the adult produce the smooth ground-down surface on the back teeth, so noticeable in our country among the labouring classes, and in the jaws of skulls of ancient Britons which are occasionally dug up.

The bot-fly (Œstrus) is an occasional source of annoyance. It lays its egg under the skin of human beings, as well as of animals, and the egg becomes in due course a maggot; the swelling resulting from the growth of the creature producing the most intense itching, which is only relieved by the escape of the maggot, either through an opening which occurs by ulceration, or through an artificial one made by the lancet.

* 'Specificity and Evolution in Disease,' by W. J. Collins, M.D. London: H. K. Lewis, Gower Street.

The wood-tick (Ixodes) is a much more frequent nuisance. It hangs in thousands upon the grass stalks along every path, and from these transfers itself to passing men and animals. Once attached, it fixes itself on by means of its forceps, and commences to suck the blood of its victim, gradually distending until the little tick which, originally, was the size and shape of a bug, soon becomes the size and shape of a gooseberry, with two depressions left to indicate where the eyes were, and a row of little pits, at the bottom of which are the legs; a hideous, repulsive bag of blood, which bursts on very slight provocation.

Even the flea, harmless enough in England, becomes a source of the most extreme discomfort when it swarms in countless millions, as it does in some badly-kept huts. The only way to get rid of it is to turn out the whole place; sweep the floors and sprinkle them with kerosine, and clean and sprinkle every article before returning it to its place. After two or three repetitions of this treatment, the plague ceases, not to return in a well-kept hut.

Lung affections are very common amongst the natives. The sudden changes of temperature in the rainy season, with no corresponding change in garments, naturally induces these conditions. A native will easily succumb to an attack once induced, as the causes which induced it will also increase it. Lung affections, secondary to malarial fever, are a very fruitful source of death to natives suffering from what would otherwise be a by no means serious attack of the fever. The same conditions which incite lung complaints, also tend to the prevalence of rheumatism; which, however, is rarely very acute. Heart-disease and dropsy are not uncommon.

Worms are a very frequent source of trouble to children; and so are their sequelæ met with in England.

The native method of grinding corn, between two soft stones, naturally produces a mixture of meal and stone dust, and the porridge made from this is often eaten by Europeans as well as natives. It never seems to injure the native when healthy, and frequently does not injure the healthy European; but when suffering from dysentery or typhoid, this food is distinctly harmful, even for the native, and to my knowledge has often caused death. I believe it is unwise for a European to eat food made from native meal, whilst he is travelling during his first year in the tropics; after that period he will be able to judge for himself. But if he has once suffered from dysentery or typhoid, it certainly is his safest course to refrain ever after from the use of such food. At the coast, the method of grinding corn being different, the same rule does not hold good; but then at the coast American flour is plentiful, and cheap, and so the European is not tempted there to make shift with native meal.

I do not recollect having seen goître in the interior; but at the coast mild cases of the disease are of not infrequent occurrence. The soil of the coast, in those parts, at least, with which I am familiar, is composed of fossiliferous limestone, and the water of the surface wells and streams is naturally impregnated with the salts of lime, and with the other salts which are associated with lime.

It was always a surprise to me how babies in Africa could stand the treatment to which they were subjected. They are fed from birth upwards upon gruel in addition to their natural food. On theoretical grounds the majority of them should die from gastric irritation; but such does not appear to be the case, and most survive this utter neglect of the rules of physiology and dietetics. At the same time, it is very difficult to ascertain what is the death-rate amongst very young children; their deaths being a matter of such complete unimportance, that the

European would never hear of it, even if half their number were swept off by an epidemic. I was very seldom called in to see sick babies, until the natives began to understand that I would come willingly to see them, and take trouble about their infantile disorders.

There are two strange conditions, one can hardly call them diseases—albinism and melanism. Congenital abnormalities they are, strictly speaking. Albinism consists in the entire absence of pigment from the skin and appendages, so that the eyes destitute of pigment in front have a pinkish appearance, due to the blood vessels at the back of the eye showing through; the skin from the same cause has a delicate pink hue; the parts of the body usually pigmented are not so, and the hair is perfectly white. This condition, familiar to us in England amongst men, usually in the person of some friend or acquaintance, is also well-known to us amongst animals in the shape of white rats; and if we frequent museums, in the shape of white starlings, white bullfinches, and white sparrows. Strange to say, it occurs amongst the Africans; so that we have the almost repulsive sight of a man with pure negro features, white woolly hair, and a perfectly white skin, the albino negro, the gazing stock and jest of the negro world. In melanism, just the opposite condition holds. Black sheep are familiar to all dwellers in the country; black rabbits, squirrels, and leopards to frequenters of museums; but melanism apparently never occurs amongst man, so that the albino negro has no corresponding abnormal brother amongst the white races.

The absence of cold in Central Africa makes an enormous difference in the sufferings amongst the poor there and in England. After working amongst the poor in England, and living amongst the scenes of slavery in Central Africa, I certainly feel that the misery and pain suffered by the natives of Africa is not to be compared with the misery, pain, and sorrow that exist amongst the very poor in all our great cities, especially during the winter months.

CHAPTER VI

THE TRAVELLER

VERY few are the favoured individuals who arrive in East Africa with a clear idea of what they are likely to encounter, or provided with half of the necessaries of comfortable, if even of actual existence. It is very difficult for a man who has always lived in a civilized country to realize what his condition will be like when he has no shops within one or two months' journey, or to remember every item which he ought to lay in for an absence of perhaps one or two years. Mr. Ashe, in his deeply-interesting book 'Two Kings of Uganda,' says: 'I may mention some of the mistakes which were made: we were provided with Epsom salts by the stone, but found ourselves short of common table-salt. Our large supply of castor-oil was but a poor compensation for the entire absence of such a necessity as butter, and for my part I would gladly have exchanged our elaborate distilling apparatus for another common tea-kettle.'

Briefly, the traveller who proposes to penetrate into the interior of Central Africa must be prepared to live without the certainty of fresh supplies, except meat, for the whole time he may be absent; for though the probability is that he will be able to purchase other food, it is possible that he may not be able to do so for days or even weeks together. His luggage must be made up into loads of such a size and weight as to be easily carried by his porters on their heads or shoulders. He must be prepared to walk the whole way himself, reserving his hammock for his carriage during sickness; and he and his men must also be well armed, for the better armed he is, the less likelihood there is of his arms being needed. Lastly, he must have a very large supply of both patience and firmness if his journey is to be really successful.

Until quite lately it was at Zanzibar that all travellers made ready their caravans; but the establishment of the Imperial British East Africa Company at Mombasa has made that port an important base from which caravans are sent into the interior.

Zanzibar has quite an imposing effect viewed from

a steamer. The white solid-looking houses stand out well in relief against the sea in front and the green palm-trees behind. Approaching nearer you see that one long street fronts the sea, behind which are some of the principal houses—the French Hotel to the north, and the British Consulate and Agency to the south. In the middle is a large square, at the back of which is the Sultan's old palace; and at the time I first visited it (1886) his only one. It looks not unlike a large doll's house, and is ornamented with semicircular windows with alternate panes of bright blue and bright green. To the north of the palace are the Sultan's ironworks, and between these two places some waste ground, on which lie in wild profusion portions of cannon, boilers, steam-trams, engines, and other rusting remains, behind which rises a plastered building with green window-shutters in various stages of degeneration, in keeping with the crumbling, eaten surface of the once white-plastered walls. This factory-like structure is the town-house of the Sultan's harem. The greater part of the remainder of the town is composed of far inferior houses to the rather massive-looking structures which front the sea. The streets are so narrow that in many places you can touch both side-walls at once. They are gutters as well as streets, as it is the custom in Zanzibar to throw your refuse out of your windows; whilst beneath each window there is a hole in the stone floor of the room which leads out into the street, and down which is poured your dirty water. A careful servant would look to see if there were passers-by before commencing to do this; but Zanzibar servants are not all careful.

Two days after my arrival at Zanzibar the great fast of Ramadan was over, and all the natives appeared in clean garments. The native costume consists of a white garment exactly like an embroidered nightshirt. And very nice and neat it looks when clean. The Sultan held a reception in honour of the day; and in the morning, quite early, received the English residents. We assembled at Sir John Kirk's house, and then marched in procession to the new palace, which was not quite finished. As we entered, the band, composed of Egyptians, played 'God save the Queen.' Then we marched upstairs, and were received at the top by his Highness, who gave a hearty shake of the hands to each, after which we went into the reception-room—a long room with white-plastered walls and a blue dado. The floor was covered with a thick warm carpet with a flaring pattern. Between the windows, on

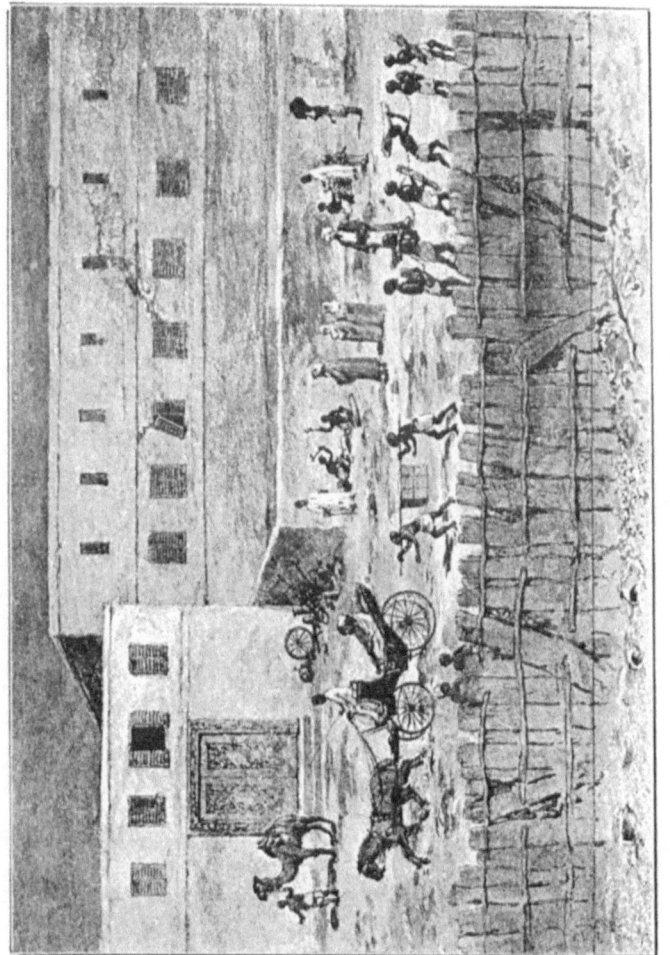

THE ESPLANADE, ZANZIBAR.

the walls, were splendid mirrors, whilst down the sides of the room were settees and chairs in velvet and gilt, and very comfortable they were. Presently the Sultan came in and sat on a chair of state, with Sir John on his right. Then barefooted attendants appeared and brought us sweetmeats, which to our English palates tasted nasty, and sherbet (nastier), and next coffee in golden cups, which would have been excellent but that the cups were half filled with barley sugar; lastly, attar of roses was brought to perfume our handkerchiefs with. Then the Sultan rose and went to the door, gave each of us another hearty shake of the hands, and we departed.

But to return to the wants of the traveller. When brought face to face with a list of the necessaries for a year's absence from civilization, one stands fairly aghast at the multitude of odds and ends which are required, and one realizes the number of people upon whom one is dependent when living even the quietest life at home. Happy the man who does stand aghast at the list of things which he has to take, instead of, as is too often the case six months later, mournfully discovering the number of necessaries which he has forgotten to bring.

Most of his outfit the thoughtful European will have purchased before he went out; but certain portions he will have wisely left until his arrival at Zanzibar, chief amongst these being the barter articles. Wherever one goes throughout Central Africa, cloth is the standard article of barter—it is the current coin; and common coarse calico is the kind of cloth which is everywhere in demand, whatever the particular fashion of the place may be as to coloured and fancy cloths. This article, therefore, he will have to lay in literally by the mile. It is sold in bales of thirty to forty yards each; and five or six of these bales, making a total of one hundred and eighty or two hundred yards, are tightly packed in cord, and then sewn up in matting, constituting one man's load. About two yards of this calico is the weekly allowance to each porter for the purchase of his food, which is the only thing allowed him on the march, his wages being paid partly in advance, and partly on his return to Zanzibar. This measure of a fathom is known by the natives as an *upande*, and the supply of food which it is supposed to purchase is called *posho*. Wire and beads make up the remainder of the recognised barter articles, but knives, soap, salt, small mirrors, thread, needles, tobacco, and especially sweetmeats, are very useful for occasional barter, and for purchasing inexpensive products. They constitute, in fact, the small change of Africa, the smallest quantity of cloth usually salable being about the value of a quarter dollar. The knives used for barter should be made of iron or soft steel, as the natives cannot sharpen good steel, and are apt to break it. The soap should be good—except for its expense, Pears' soap is undoubtedly the best for the purpose, as its value unfortunately is recognised by many of the natives. Indeed Mandara, the Sultan of Kilimanjaro, always insists upon having Pears' when you barter soap with him. 'I want the sort you can see through,' he remarks, when you endeavour to pass off another article upon him, and there is nothing for it but to give up some of your own toilet-soap, or go without what you want to obtain. It is strange how some of our household articles in England get a reputation in savage lands. I remember a traveller on one occasion presenting a tablet of Pears' soap to an unwashed chief who had brought him a present of a very scraggy fowl, and who refused it—a very rude thing for a chief to do, as he knew better manners than that. 'You call yourself a big chief,' said the traveller, 'you are only a little chief; every big chief knows this soap.' He was very hard up for food at the time, and had hardly any articles of barter left, so that the rejection of his soap, where he had expected that it would take well, no doubt sharpened his remarks. But though it is advisable to take good soap for chiefs and other big folk, it is very necessary to take a large supply of common bar-soap. If to no one else, you can always get rid of it to your porters, who will manage to get things you want from the natives in exchange for it. Salt is everywhere esteemed. Commander Cameron told me that he used to purchase it when on a journey in places where it was cheap, and sell it again where it was dear; but the native salt is both dirty, which the natives do not object to; and bitter, which they do; so that good English salt is always acceptable and salable even in salt-producing districts. The same holds good of tobacco, which is best purchased in Zanzibar, and of course best disposed of in districts where tobacco is little grown. Needles and thread can only occasionally be got rid of; but they take up very little space, and when they can be disposed of will save a more valuable article ot barter. Sweetmeats are exceedingly useful, especially for inducing boys to work; but one or two must be given away to stimulate their appetite and so create the demand for these articles. The hard marble-like sweetmeats are especially useful, as a group of boys will pass one round, and each extract the juice for a minute; and so one sweetmeat stimulates a number of palates, and thus creates a proportionate demand for more.

Some men are much quicker than others in obtaining reasonable terms from the natives. Ashe was always very successful this way, he rarely failed, but I remember one instance of his doing so. He had been bargaining with a young man, who at a time when we were in great straits for food agreed to purchase Ashe's waistcoat for an amount of food equal to two shillings, but instead of bringing the food, he returned the waistcoat shortly after, with the crushing remark that it was not worth it. About that time, too, I emptied out the contents of my medicine-chest, and Ashe sold the empty bottles as snuff-boxes. His usual plan was, after having dilated upon its capabilities, to sell a bottle for one or two days' supply of vegetables, or a dozen eggs. After the bargain was concluded and the purchaser had departed, Ashe used to call him back again, show him a cork, and dilate upon its capabilities for closing a bottle, and the result usually was some more vegetables or three more eggs.

It is always safest in preparing for a journey to consider that you may be able to get nothing but meat and eggs, and occasionally not even these. Take, therefore, just sufficient supplies of biscuit, flour, sugar, tea, coffee, condensed milk, tinned butter, tinned lard and oatmeal for the whole period, and a sufficient supply of delicacies for a two months' illness.

As regards clothing, hats and helmets are best purchased in Zanzibar. The pith helmets sold there have wider brims than the ones obtainable in India, or at the outfitters' at home. For clothing, the best for everyday wear is perhaps an ordinary tweed suit made without lining. For travelling some prefer kakee canvas suits, others cricketing flannels and a thick blazer with a spinal pad. Flannels are more apt to get torn than the canvas, but they are much more comfortable, warmer in the chilly morning air, and cooler under the blazing sun. Waterproof leggings are most useful for the early morning in the marshy districts, before the sun has evaporated the very heavy dew which collects every night on the grass and bushes; and they can be taken off directly the grass gets dry. A policeman's cape will protect the coat in going through high grass under the same conditions. Boots are usually worn with very square toes and thick soles, unblackened, natural brown leather being the material. The thick soles answer a double purpose; they prevent the sharp inequalities of the rough uneven mountain paths being felt by the feet, and also prevent the hot baked rocks or scorching sand, over which the traveller often has to march for miles, from blistering the soles of his feet. If away from the coast for a long time together, we used to take extra soles with us, ready made to fit, pierced with holes, and provided with a supply of appropriate nails. The boot to be mended was placed on an ordinary last, having a thin metal sole screwed on to it; and the old leather sole was cut off from the boot, and the new one, previously soaked in water for twenty-four hours, nailed on in its place, well hammered down, and the edges then trimmed with a knife; in one, or at most two days, the sole was dry again and hard, and the boot ready for use.

One mistake frequently made by the inexperienced traveller, into which he is led by the outfitter at home, is to sacrifice utility and strength to imaginary portability in his tent furniture and cooking pots. To this end the tent and bed poles are made in sections, resulting in a great weakening of their structure, and rendering them more awkward as loads, for the porter has perhaps three pieces of three feet each to tie together every morning, usually with the scantiest supply of cord, instead of one convenient pole nine feet long, which he can easily balance, easily carry, and which he has not the trouble of tying and untying each day. From the same mistaken notion the utility of saucepans and kettles is sometimes impaired. Ordinary stout English articles are by far the best, as they can be bundled into a basket each day, and easily carried in this way. Portable handles are convenient for losing, but for no other purpose.

After having carefully made up all his baggage into loads of sixty pounds each, and having provided a corresponding number of porters, with one headman for each ten men, and a cook and boy for himself, the traveller is ready to leave Zanzibar for the mainland. A traveller who wished to manage things economically, yet with safety, and not to be absent more than three months, nor travel more than six hundred miles, could manage comfortably with thirty men, and, as these on an average would cost him, all incidental expenses included, less than thirty shillings a month each, the total cost of such an expedition, exclusive of his own outfit, and the English food he took with him would be under one hundred and thirty-five pounds, probably under one hundred pounds. After such an experience as this he would know how and where to economise, and what amount of roughing he could stand. I once travelled two hundred miles in ten days, with no discomforts, except being tired, and occasionally footsore, at a total cost of seven pounds; whilst Mr. Ashe on one occasion came from the Victoria Nyanza to the coast, nearly eight hundred miles, for about ten pounds; but he had both discomforts and hardships to endure. These figures will show what *can* be done; but it needs experience—and nothing else will take its place—to travel economically in Central Africa.

The first time that I left Zanzibar for the interior, we started by dhow at mid-day, and arrived at Saadani at sunset. With truly oriental indifference the captain of the dhow had no boat on board in which to land us, nor had he provided one at Saadani to be sent to meet us; so he grounded his dhow, and calmly waited until the ebbing tide should leave her high and dry. Meanwhile it had become dark, and I was getting hungry, so that there was nothing for it but to swim ashore, and soon I was safe in a mud hut enjoying tea. There were plenty of mosquitoes there, as there are at all seasons along the coast swamp; but they did not trouble me much;

perhaps my prolonged sea-sickness had impaired my flavour.

Whilst at Saadani I received a visit from some Wanyamwezi, who had come down with a large caravan from the interior. They came into my hut and sat in a semicircle on the ground, and after having cleaned their teeth with a piece of stick broken up into fibres at the end, and tried to soil my mud floor by spitting upon it, they commenced conversation. I could only understand one question put by the leading man. It related to a structure which evidently was new to his experience. ' Bwana (*master*),' he said, in an interested tone, ' how much did your trousers cost ?'

Saadani or some other coast town being the starting point for the march into the interior, the porters here receive their food-money or posho for three days in advance, at the rate of five pice (five farthings) a day each man. For the first ten marches from the coast the natives will take pice in payment, beyond that distance cloth. At the start a day is quite taken up in paying the posho, dividing the loads, hiring new porters to replace those who have failed at the last moment, and making all final arrangements. The next day the start up country is usually made.

PAYING POSHO.

It is light about half-past five in the morning, and we usually started as soon after this as possible; breakfast finished, tents struck, and everything packed up before six. Marching has to be done in Indian file, the paths being very narrow, and occasionally so hollowed in the centre, that one foot has to be placed immediately in front of the other, rendering walking in such places rather awkward and very fatiguing.

Near the villages the ground is generally cultivated, millet, Indian corn, and sweet potatoes being the chief products on the first plateau. Millet or Indian corn made into a stiff porridge called 'ugali' formed the staple article of food of our native porters on caravan journeys. The head-men, who had better pay than the rank and file, occasionally bought a goat and divided it, though they preferred our buying a goat and making them presents of joints. The porters, unable to afford goats, were in most places able to buy chickens to eat with their ugali. These they plucked, cleaned, split open, and dried, giving them much the appearance of kippered herrings; and prepared in this way, they would last many days.

The men divided themselves into sets or camps of five or six each, in this way saving themselves much trouble in their commissariat arrangements. One did the cooking, two or three fetched fuel and water and went to the nearest village to barter for food, whilst the others built the hut for the night—made like an Indian wigwam, the framework being of sticks, and the covering of long grass—which was as dry as straw, and nearly as strong.

I was very much surprised at the good behaviour of the men. Sometimes there would be not one single case of squabbling during an entire march, if one could judge from their tones and expressions. Yet they were heathen, all of them; for although some of them considered themselves Mohammedans, they were so only in name.

Not long after starting on my first journey up country, I was laid low with fever, brought on, I have no doubt now, from drinking unboiled water in a malarious district through which for a few marches we passed; and so I was obliged to continue the journey by hammock, a very luxurious method of travelling. I was always glad when the time came for exchanging the hard camp-bed for the comfort and ease of the yielding hammock. Very careful the men were with their sick charge. One man ran in front of the hammock to see that there were no boughs projecting in the way; whilst in crossing the streams four men would go with us, two on each side, and joining their hands under the hammock raise it well out of reach of the water.

The East African paths which have been referred to before, and which are called for euphony roads, are very interesting but very tiring features of the country. Every village is connected with its neighbours by means of these paths, which thus run right across Africa, the main paths frequented by the trans-continental caravans being slightly wider, distinctly smoother, and more bare of vegetation than the less-frequented routes. The traveller is thus rarely at a loss as to the way, the coast-porters knowing all the chief routes up to the lakes, and the natives of each district, easily obtainable as guides from camp to camp, knowing all the by-paths. These paths are wonderfully sinuous, and Professor Drummond gives an account of the chief methods by which they originate. He must have observed very carefully, as his account is very accurate, and, considering the short time he was in Africa, very complete. I have watched natives making roads between two villages, and have occasionally helped in endeavouring to find short cuts between villages. Wherever the ground is fairly even, and uncovered by brushwood or thorns, there the native makes his path in a direct line towards his goal; but unfortunately this is only occasionally the condition, and he is thus driven to make circuitous routes, taking advantage of every furrow and cleared space worn by the temporary streams which are originated each rainy season, and, to a larger extent, following the innumerable wild beast tracks which cross and intercross with wonderful complexity, covering every square mile of the Continent. Thus, without axe or pick, and with only the occasional use of the billhook, a native will find a path from any one point to any other. Once started, the path, never very straight, soon becomes still more circuitous on account of fortuitous circumstances. Every strong wind in Africa brings down some tree which has lived out its allotted span, and some of these will necessarily fall across the road. Now, to a native with a load, a climb over a trunk not quite touching the ground, or a scramble underneath it, is not so expeditious as going round the tree, and round it he goes. Occasionally some more enterprising or thoughtful inhabitant or passer-by will start a fire in the trunk, which, if it be the dry season, will gradually smoulder for days, or even weeks, until at last a white band of ashes alone marks the position of the obstacle, and the path is restored. But more often there is no one who has time or inclination for such a deed, and the tree remains, until in the course of a year or two the white ants have eaten the sun-dried timber, and the wind and rains have broken up and scattered the fragments ; but by this time rank grass, creepers, thorns, and underwood have sprung up over the unused path, and the detour originally made to avoid the fallen tree has become part of the permanent way. Over and over again have I noticed this in passing and repassing roads at intervals of perhaps six months. Another still more frequent cause of alteration in the paths is the want of any authority to enforce respect for a recognised right-of-way. For two or three miles round each village the inhabitants have their farms or shambas, and it frequently suits a man's convenience to take the public road into his shamba ; so forthwith he ploughs it up, and digs it into deep furrows and ridges, which would effectually prevent the traveller attempting it twice, if the strong thorn barrier, which at the same time the occupier erects round his shamba, did not prevent his doing it once. Often at the beginning of the cultivating season have I suddenly found myself obliged to go out of my way for two or three hundred yards on account of the thoughtless selfishness of some African husbandman. Sometimes in the plains the heavy rains of an unusually wet season will make some path so soft and heavy that a new one has to be temporarily made; but the old path thus released from traffic, and at the same time softened by the rains, is rapidly covered with vegetation and hidden from sight, and so, even when the rains are over, it is disused and soon forgotten. Such a path is said to have 'died.' Only for the purposes of strategy, and then but rarely, will natives go to the trouble of using axe and hoe to make a new path. I have known such a path, ending abruptly in the jungle a hundred yards from the main road, for secrecy's sake, made across a long distance in a very short time.

The distance a caravan marches daily is limited chiefly by the loads, ten miles a day being a fair average with sixty-pound loads; but the distance must always be determined by the water supplies. If there is no water for thirty miles at a stretch, it is best to march the whole of that distance in one day, or, better still, in one night; but if the distance is greater, one day's supply of water may be taken, and the journey done in two days. But taking water adds, of course, to the burdens to be carried, and diminishes the distance it is possible to march.

With thirty-pound loads it is quite possible to march twenty miles a day, six days a week, without unduly fatiguing Europeans or carriers. A heavier load, if really necessary, can be carried on a pole by two men; but a load of only fifty pounds would be carried by two men, who separately would carry thirty pounds each; and a load of ninety-five pounds is all that will be carried, without incessant bother and grumbling, by two men, who separately would carry sixty pounds each. In this respect certain tribes differ. The Wanyamwezi will both carry heavier loads than the Zanzibaris, and also a heavier proportionate double load. They will also carry what is known as the 'madala,' which consists of two thirty-pound loads slung one at each end of a pole. This is often a convenient load for a traveller, and things so packed can be carried more safely and carefully than in the ordinary way.

The Wanyamwezi, who occupy a large tract in the interior south of the Victoria Nyanza and east of Tanganyika, are the great traders and carriers of Central Africa. Mr. Ashe, who knows them even better than I do, says:

'. . . . in spite of certain things which I could not but dislike about these people, they showed so many fine qualities that they won my sincerest admiration.

Patience, fortitude, strong affection, dogged perseverance were their better characteristics.'

As a tribe I liked them better than any other that I came across. They are excellent carriers; but when travelling it is, I think, best to have both Zanzibaris and Wanyamwezi in the caravan, each under their respective head-men and independent of the other, except that an Arab or half-Arab is put in charge of the entire caravan. The Zanzibaris and Wanyamwezi will make separate camps at a little distance from each other, at each resting-place; and whatever troubles arise, even such an exceptional one as we encountered, namely, war between the Germans and Arabs, they will never combine to make common cause against the white man.

The water supply, as we have seen, is the great source of anxiety on many marches. It is always well to give one or two men light loads and extra posho, so that they may keep well in front of the caravan, each carrying a bucket, and go at once on their arrival to fetch water. In this way the traveller is sure of getting water before all the porters have exhausted it temporarily, as they sometimes do, and certainly before they have stirred up the mud and polluted it; as, except in the rare case of running streams, they always do.

Neglect of Sanitation

When arranging the camping-place, it is wise to choose a spot, if possible, which will be shaded by trees in the afternoon, otherwise the heat will be almost unbearable; and, in any case, the traveller should keep well to windward of the general camp, and if there is one, on a slight elevation. It is very necessary to keep to windward of the camp, as sanitary observances are painfully neglected both by Zanzibaris and Wanyamwezi, especially by the latter. Mr. Stokes, a trader who travels only with Wanyamwezi, and lives in camp with them, can never remain at the same place over twenty-four hours; and consequently, even on Sunday, usually marches a mile or two for a very necessary 'change of air.'

When there is not time or material for building temporary huts, the porters content themselves with drawing closer to their fires, which they then keep up more carefully. The fires have the double effect of keeping them warm, and frightening away wild animals. The traveller who sleeps in his tent will need to keep the ends open for coolness' sake; and this will necessitate either his personal servants sleeping near the door, and lighting their fires there, or his keeping a small lamp burning all night at the door, or, what is best of all, having a dog there on guard. A mastiff, a bull-dog, or a large bull-terrier is a match for any animal except a lion, and would give timely notice of the approach of the latter.

I always endeavoured to take small tents for my servants and head-men, in addition to my own tent, especially if they had their wives with them. A small tente d'abri made of strong twill, measuring about five feet by six feet at the base and four feet six inches high, capable of holding three people in the way that the natives pack at night, can be made for five or six shillings; and, with two bamboo-poles and six tent-pegs complete, will weigh less than six pounds. To each servant and head-man I also gave, when obtainable, a blanket. Apart from all other reasons, it is good policy to look carefully after the health of your servants and head-men. For this purpose an extra tent, and one or two extra blankets and warm vests, in case of sickness amongst the other porters, are also advisable. Most of the men, when sick, will come along with the caravan, and often carry a light load, and sometimes their full load, if they are cared for when they arrive in camp. In addition to tents and clothing, it is well to set aside a small supply of arrowroot, rice, tapioca, condensed milk, sugar, coffee, and curry as medical extras for those really ill. All the preceding comforts will not cost more than three or four pounds, whilst delaying even a small caravan on account of sickness costs at least one pound a day. One frequently hears of death on the road amongst porters in the caravans; but most of the deaths, the details of which I am familiar with, have been caused by ignorance or neglect on the part of the leaders.

Except in cases where it is probable that the journey will be prolonged through the dry season only, it is wiser to take a large sheet of green Willesden canvas with eyelets and loops at intervals along the edge. This is very useful in wet weather as a covering for the loads; and if the loads be carefully stacked up in the centre, there will be plenty of room for a good number of porters as well to obtain shelter underneath it.

I always took a ten-foot bamboo hammock-pole with me, as bamboo-poles are very light and strong, and but rarely obtainable up country, the poles of sufficient strength that are obtainable there being very heavy. At the camping-places this pole comes in useful as a roof-support for the luggage-tent which we have been describing.

We have not yet spoken of the system prevalent amongst some of the interior tribes of exacting toll, or as it is called *hongo* or *mhongo*, from the passing traveller. It is often the cause of a great deal of annoyance to the traveller, though, when well administered, it is a fair and sensible enough system. All through Eastern Equatorial Africa, as we have seen, the water, in the great majority of places, is only to be obtained from wells, some of which have to be sunk with a great deal of labour, considering the imperfect tools which the natives possess for the purpose; and when sunk, often yield but a scanty supply of water. The natives having the trouble of sinking these wells, it is only fair that passing caravans should pay for the privilege of using the water.

Some years ago an Arab coming down from the interior with his caravan determined that he would refuse hongo, and force his way down by strength of arms. He endeavoured to do so; no open opposition was offered to him; but the wells along the route were closed, and new ones unknown to him opened for the local needs. Only two or three of his party reached the coast alive. All the remainder died of thirst on the way.

But such a system, with no regulated tariff, is necessarily abused, and exorbitant charges are sometimes levied upon caravans; not only so, but local superstitions are made use of to swell the amount demanded by some rapacious chief. If, for instance, one of your men happens to be taken ill, you may have to pay damages; for such an event is likely to bring ill-luck to the village at which you are staying. One of my friends had once to pay a fine, because, when on a journey, he had his hair cut at a season when such observances were not permitted for fear of injuring the harvest; and another, because he took a bath in his tent at a time when bathing was prohibited for fear of stopping the rains.

Of course, a man going by force with a strong caravan across Africa, could resist such charges as the two latter; but it would hardly be wise for a missionary to do so. Practically there are two distinct methods of travelling in safety through Africa, and it is unwise to attempt to combine the two. The one method is to take a well-armed, well-organized force with you, and go, injuring no one unprovoked, by permitted roads when there are such, and only by forbidden ones when there is no alternative, and always endeavouring to come to terms before proceeding to force. The other is, to take no more arms than necessary to resist attacks from highwaymen between the villages, going only by permitted routes, paying what charges are insisted upon, or else turning back, and going into no new district without first asking, and obtaining permission from the local chief. The former is practically Stanley's method, and the method adopted by traders; the latter, Livingstone's, and the method adopted by missionaries. It is, I think, folly for any man to go into a new district without permission from the chief, and for a missionary to do so with a large force would be fatal to his work. Go by permission, and you are quite safe. The chief may ask you for presents, but your life and property are usually secure as long as you are in his district; and if you are robbed you can generally depend on his rendering justice to you, and punishment to the offender.

CHAPTER VII

A DAY'S MARCH

MORE than an hour before the first ray of dawn, the alarum woke us up, on one of our journeys, to the fact that another day's march lay before us, and that there was no time to be lost if we wished to be well on our way before the sun had risen high enough to make travelling by foot a work of utter weariness. The moon had sunk below the horizon soon after midnight, and only the faint starlight, or the occasional flicker of a camp-fire as it gradually died out, enabled us to see the dim forms of sleepers scattered on the ground all about. We heard the bark of a solitary jackal, but most other creatures had already gone back to their lairs. After waking our boy and our cook, we began to dress. The season was hot, but even tropical water seems cold in the very early morning, and travellers rarely indulge in a bath before a march, as the waiting about for the final start would probably result in their getting chilled, and this might not unlikely end in a fever. So we contented ourselves with more modest ablutions, and reserved the bath until our arrival in camp, when it would be no longer dangerous, and far more refreshing, if not also more needed. Having dressed in canvas suits, with waterproof leggings to protect ourselves against the dew-covered grass, we were ready to turn our attention to packing up our belongings for the march. This early morning packing is rather a tedious duty, as everything has to be folded carefully in order to take up little space, and all breakables have to be packed fairly tightly together in order to avoid breakage during the jolting to which they will be subjected on the march. By this time more than an hour had gone by, and there was just a suspicion of approaching light in the far east. There was a stirring amongst the sleeping forms, who began to rise, and each unwinding the sheet which had served him as bed-clothes, proceeded to fold it, and tuck it round his waist as a sort of long loin-cloth or short skirt; or else suspend it by a knot over one shoulder, and allow it to envelop him as far as his knees.

Whilst the porters were thus engaged, the boy brought us some porridge, and a cup of coffee, which he placed upon the camp-table outside the tent, and we drew our camp-stools up to it, clear of the tent, which the porters, who were told off for that purpose, now commenced to strike, and to make up into loads. The canvas of the walls and roof formed one load, the fly and tent-poles another, whilst the ground-sheet, tent-pegs and mallet, went to form part of a third. Whilst we were having our coffee, the cook rapidly washed up, and packed his cooking-pots ready for the porter who was impatiently waiting for them. The other porters, too, were busily making up their loads ready for the start; tying their cooking pots and sleeping-mats on to the outside of our packages. For this purpose, they used cord made of cocoa-nut fibre, which they had brought with them from the coast; and the finding of their various pieces, which they had carelessly thrown about the night before, the desire of the men with small allowances of cord to exchange them for the longer pieces lying temptingly near, and the still greater eagerness of the men with no cord at all to annex any small pieces which lay near at hand, usually resulted in a good deal of noise, and a certain amount of quarrelling, not unmixed with bursts of laughter, as some unfortunate man, who usually had six yards of rope, pathetically held up a miserable two feet, which had been substituted for his treasured length. One or two of the men refreshed themselves with ugali; but the majority preferred to go empty, and wait until their day's march was over, when they would be able to rest, and eat their food at leisure.

There was now sufficient light to enable us to start, and we were just about to do so, when we were delayed by the refusal of a Zanzibari, named Kasembi, to continue to carry the valise in which our blankets were packed, and which was consequently a rather bulky load, although it only weighed fifty pounds. Happily, we were able to settle the matter by giving him a small case weighing seventy pounds, which an Mnyamwezi was carrying (the Wanyamwezi carry heavier loads than the Zanzibaris), and which the Zanzibari preferred to the valise, whilst the Mnyamwezi was equally pleased to exchange it for the other's lighter load; so that we were not delayed many minutes.

Most of the more active men had now started, and the hammock-bearers, who carried my wife, took up their burden without further delay, and went away at a merry trot along the narrow path. The boy came with us, as the short delay had enabled him to finish washing up the plates and mugs which we had just used, and to pack them away in their proper basket.

Usually he started later, and had to catch us up, as he carried with him my gun, telescope and water-bottle, articles which might be needed during the march. One head-man went on with the first detachment, but the chief head-man remained behind to see that all the loads were safely taken off, after doing which, he walked at the rear of the column to see that no stragglers fell out on the march with their loads. He had to remain longer than usual to-day, as one of the men had gone the previous evening to a neighbouring village, where the villagers were brewing beer from millet seed, and had indulged so freely, that he was helplessly drunk, and quite unable to carry his load. This necessitated a villager being engaged to carry it as far as the next camp, for the sum of two yards of calico, a corresponding amount being struck off the wages of the defaulter.

The hammock-bearers went along at such a swinging pace, that one by one we gradually caught up and passed the different porters. The first whom we passed was a very spruce-looking Zanzibari, dressed in comparatively clean calico, who rejoiced in the not very appropriate, and certainly not very flattering name of Mjinga (the simpleton). Next to him came two boys, Mulandu and Mafundo, about sixteen and seventeen years of age respectively, carrying one ordinary load of sixty pounds between them on a pole. Young though they were, they got along bravely each day. It is surprising what long marches even children in Africa will make. There was a little boy of eight years old on a march with us once, and though we happened to be making rather long marches—twenty to twenty-four miles daily—yet he very rarely needed to be carried.

The dress of two other men was somewhat conspicuous. One wore an old nightshirt discarded by some European traveller, as his overall, and another some left off underlinen which he had obtained at the coast, and which might have passed for white knickerbockers, but for the frill of embroidery.

Well on, along the line, was Bundula, a very active man, who usually kept almost at the head of the column. He was an Mnyamwezi, who had lost his right hand by a gun accident many years before, and who yet managed to carry his madala load (two loads tied on at opposite ends of a pole), and to tie it up most skilfully every morning, notwithstanding this defect.

After two hours' march the sun had risen sufficiently high to evaporate the dew which had hitherto lain so thickly on the grass, and I was glad to take off my long heavy gaiters. Shortly after this the boy pointed out to us some giraffes in the distance. They were about a mile away, and were going very fast, but evidently at, to them, quite an easy trot. The brushwood about here was comparatively low, and there were very few trees, so that the movements of the whole herd could be seen very plainly, there being nothing capable of giving them concealment. Near this we passed the spoor of a lion and giraffe side by side; evidently the former had been chasing the latter, but had not succeeded in catching him. The ground was hard, and the spoor not very distinct; but had it been the rainy season, and the ground soft and marshy, the lion would not improbably have been successful, as under such circumstances the long feet of the giraffe would have sunk deeply into the ground at each stride, and greatly impaired his progress.

As we journeyed on we noticed a native pipe and water gourd hanging from the bough of a tree, and asked what it was there for. 'It is a wizard's place of execution,' we were told. 'They burnt him under the tree, and then hung up his property in it as a warning to others.' Just here the path divided, and one of the hammock-bearers placed a twig across the wrong path, to warn the porters who followed against going by it. This was very necessary, especially as it was the usual path, which had become blocked further on, 'had died' as the natives would have said; and it was necessary to go for some distance by the new track, which by a detour of half a mile led finally into the old one. The men nearest us would have seen which way we went, and followed easily; but the caravan was so scattered, extending over more than a mile, that some of the men would arrive at the division of ways when there was no longer anyone in sight ahead of them. It would be dangerous to scatter in this way far in the interior; but for the first two hundred miles from the coast there is practically little danger, and men often travel with only one companion, and sometimes with none.

We had now arrived nearly at the mid point of our journey, and as it was a rather longer march than usual, we had intended to rest half way at a stream which flowed partly round a small conical hill that had enormous boulders down its sides and at its base. We had hoped to find water here; but unfortunately the stream was quite dry, so that we were disappointed of the half-hour's rest, and the tea which we intended to have made. We always took with us for this purpose a small flat kettle, which

An Unusually Hot Day

would rapidly have boiled over a quickly-made fire of twigs and dried leaves. We had to content ourselves with some lukewarm water from the flask which the boy carried, and a rest of ten minutes; as it was hardly fair to delay the hammock-bearers at a place where they could get no water.

An hour later we arrived at a comparatively large stream, which flowed all through the dry season; and here the men refreshed themselves by drinking, and some of them by bathing. It is surprising what a small amount of water satisfies a thirsty native. After a long march without water, under a fierce sun he will content himself with a few sips. I suppose long practice in husbanding his supplies of water enables him to do this. We did not stop long here, as we were anxious to finish our journey, for it was getting towards the hottest part of an unusually hot day. I was glad of the shelter of an umbrella in addition to the protection afforded by a pith helmet; and all the porters who had spare pieces of cloth about them made them into turbans, audibly lamenting the heat, as they walked along perspiring under their loads. Although I had no load I longed for camp, but did not know how far off it was. In answer to our inquiries the men kept saying 'karibu, karibu' (close, close); but natives are not good at estimating distances accurately, and still worse at expressing their estimates. They often began to say 'karibu' when the end was yet five miles off.

The way now led through rather more closely-wooded country, and the path became a tunnel through the lofty thorn bushes which interlaced and met overhead, so close above our heads in places, that many of the porters kept knocking their loads against the boughs, and one who was running along rather incautiously was knocked clean off his feet by his load being caught against an overhanging branch. The thorn-bushes, too, were so close together, and the path so very winding, that it was often difficult to get the long ten-foot hammock-pole round the sharp turnings, without the bearer at one end or the other being pushed into the bushes. To add to the difficulties of the march, the way now lay up hill, and the path was very rocky and irregular; but soon we reached the summit, and shortly afterwards emerged upon a large clearing, with many coppices scattered over it. Half hidden by one of these coppices, some hundred and fifty yards away, was a herd of twenty or thirty antelope. We were in front of the caravan, but the rest at the dry stream bed, and the delay at the nearer stream, where some of the men had bathed, had allowed time for the stragglers to come up, so that the caravan had pulled itself together, and made a fairly compact body. I fired at one of the antelope, and the bullet struck it in the back, but without doing much immediate injury. The sound of the firing startled the herd, who looked this way and that for the best way to retreat. Meanwhile, one or two of us ran round one of the coppices and began to approach them unperceived, until the herd, catching sight of us, became bewildered, and scattered in different directions. Two of them passed near us, but I only had a shot cartridge in my other barrel, and so was unable to bring my animal down, though I emptied the charge into it at a distance of only ten yards. Half a dozen animals in their bewilderment rushed straight through the caravan. Dozens of guns were fired at them, many at only a few paces distance; but with the exception of one animal, which was struck in the head by a random shot from my boy, not a single other one was wounded; and to my great surprise, none of the porters either, notwithstanding the reckless fusillade from nearly two score of guns. The one animal shot in the head rushed on a few paces and then fell dead, and the Zanzibaris at once cut its throat. When we came to cut it up and examine it, we found that it was the same animal which I had shot in the back, and that it had also received my charge of buckshot in the side. It took very few minutes to skin and cut up the animal, and distribute it amongst the caravan. Two or three pounds of meat for each porter was a luxury not obtained every day, so that everyone was in good spirits, and the heat and weariness were forgotten in the last few miles march into camp.

We had not gone far, when three guns in rapid succession informed us that the mail-men from the interior were just ahead of us. We stopped as they came up, and found some letters from our friends in the way-bag, and then looking over the way-bill, saw that amongst other packages was one from Emin Pasha. The Pasha generally managed to get one packet of letters sent down to the coast every four or five months by the Church Missionary Society's mail-men from Uganda to Zanzibar. One of these men had his cooking-pot bound up tightly behind in his loin-cloth—a very common method of carrying this article, but one which gave the wearer a decidedly peculiar appearance. We only delayed the mail-men a few minutes as we received our letters from them, and gave them our packages for

Kigwamwanzila. 199

the coast, and soon we were both on our respective ways again—they for Zanzibar, and we for the far interior. As we left them, the fact that we were approaching a village became more and more evident by the frequent clearings, signs of farms that had been or were shortly to be, and by the occasional patches of cultivated ground. Soon the village itself came into sight, and by eleven o'clock our march was over for the day.

The hammock-bearers stopped about a hundred yards from the village; and when, after searching, we had settled upon two level clearings for our tents, we were glad to sit down on the ground and rest ourselves under the friendly shade of the broad trunk of a leafless tree as we watched the loads come slowly in; though not by any means so slowly as usual, the delays on the road having, as we have seen, helped to pull the caravan together. One of the last to come in was an Mnyamwezi boy of seventeen, who rejoiced in the name of Kigwamwanzila, usually shortened into Kigwa by his friends. He was afflicted with a diseased ankle-joint, but managed to get along satisfactorily all the same. His load, however, only consisted of one or two dozen eggs, and my spare pith helmet. This last article he used to wear when I was not looking, or when he thought that I was not, and he finally returned it to me, showing unpleasant traces of contact with his unwashed head. But the last of all, were two Wanyamwezi, who had tied their two loads of sixty pounds each together, and transformed it into an unusually heavy double load, supported on a pole between them. A single load is sometimes seventy pounds in weight, a double one is rarely more than half as much again; and though these two men preferred a double load between them to a single one each, they soon found out that they had made a mistake in this instance; and next day I noticed that the loads were separated, and that each man was carrying his own on his shoulder. The Wanyamwezi always carry their loads on their shoulders, the Zanzibaris usually on the head.

The head-man did not appear after these two, as under ordinary circumstances he would have done; and on making inquiry, we found that he had remained behind to look after the load of a man who had been too poorly to carry it, and had sent on word that another porter was to come back and relieve him. An hour later he appeared with the relief, who was carrying the load.

Whilst we were resting, the porter who carried the buckets had gone off to the well some half mile away to fetch water, and the cook and boy had lighted a fire and were getting our breakfast ready. The ground where we wished to pitch our tents was rather irregular, and had thorns scattered about; but a kindly native, who was hoeing his little plot of ground near, came and cleared and levelled it for us with his hoe. The men now pitched the tents, and we were glad to get under shelter, for the sun was getting higher and higher, and the trunk of the tree, in consequence, giving us less and less shade.

We always endeavoured to pitch our tents some distance from the villages, as we did in this instance. It gave us much more privacy, a choice of shady places which could not be found inside a village, and saved us from the noise and smell of the vicinity of the huts; but during the disturbed time which followed the commencement of hostilities between the Germans and Arabs on the east coast, when no white man's life was safe, we had to forego these advantages, and camp in the safety secured by the village stockade.

A native now came up to us, bringing some eggs and a gourd of milk for sale. We were delighted at the thought of fresh milk—a delicacy not often obtained on the march; but our delight was short-lived, for when we came to examine the contents of the gourd, we found it quite sour and clotted. With the eggs we were more successful. The boy tested them by putting them in a basin of water, and rejecting those that would not lie quietly at the bottom. Finally, we bought ten of the good ones, which had stood this test, and for them we paid one yard of cloth. This bartering over, we retired to our tents, bathed and changed into flannels, and having done so, felt quite fresh again and ready for our breakfast, or rather dinner, for what we had did duty for both. It consisted of a fowl, which had been killed and roasted whilst still warm, of sweet potatoes, bread and banana fritters; and it would have been very enjoyable but for the water, which at this village was very bad. We boiled it as usual, and left it to stand, but it would not settle much even then; and the boiling, by making an infusion of the mud, had rendered the taste worse than before, so that even filtering would not greatly have improved its flavour; and this we did not like to even attempt for fear of blocking the filter. The proper way to purify such water as this, is to stir up a teaspoonful or two of alum in a bucketful, and allow the liquor to stand; then when the alum has thrown down the organic matter, to pour the clear upper layer of fluid into a kettle and boil; and finally to filter, which will not only further purify, but also partially aërate it again, and so render it less insipid. But this process would have been much too long for us to have carried out on the march, so we contented ourselves with endeavouring to disguise the taste by making it into coffee, or by adding lime-juice, and hoping for a purer supply at our next camping-place.

During the afternoon two villagers came into camp with some zebra meat which they had shot the day before. I bought a leg for our dogs, and the Wanyamwezi porters bought the remainder for their own consumption. The Zanzibaris would not touch it, as the animal had been killed by a bullet, and had not had its throat cut afterwards, so that the meat still contained the blood.

The men who had ulcers or coughs, or who were otherwise ill or thought they were, now came one by one for medicines and dressings; but they were soon disposed of, and then we were free to write up our journals for the day, or attend to the various little odds and ends connected with the housekeeping arrangements, if one may call it housekeeping when living under canvas. It was the day for baking bread, so that we had to send for the porter who carried the load of flour. He was an

Mnyamwezi, named Makolokolo; and we always had a good deal of trouble in persuading him to bring his load and unfasten it. He was not a man of very brilliant parts, and nothing would convince him that it was very much to his advantage to have his load lightened by two pounds at a time two or three times a week. The unexpected density of intellect of some amongst the interior natives—men, too, who may be sharp-witted enough on many points—renders it often a very difficult matter to deal with them fairly, without wounding their feelings, or giving them the idea that you are unjust.

The greatest annoyance which we suffered from at this camp was the ants. They were not the large kind, or siafu, which march in columns, but the very small ones, which swarm over everything and get through the tiniest crevices. They were not so bad, however, as at our previous camping-place, where they had attacked every article of food which we possessed, penetrating into every box and tin, except such as had unusually close-fitting covers. Placing a tin of butter in a saucer of water was no protection, as they quickly covered the surface of the water, and then walked over each other's floating bodies until they reached the tin. We had brought many of these ants with us in our boxes from the previous camp; but we noticed that all those that had been enclosed near the outside of the bundles or valises, or close to the surface of the metal boxes, had been killed and dried by the exposure to the great heat on the march.

As the sun was about to set, the porters who had purchased their supplies of food, and finished cooking it in the village where they were encamped, settled down in groups to their evening meal, which was the chief, often the only, one in the day. On this occasion it consisted, as usual, of ugali and kitiwayo, or relish as we should call it. The relish to-day was dried shark, which they had brought with them from Zanzibar. This shark is caught sometimes on the East African coast, but it comes chiefly from Arabia by dhow. It is sun-dried, not salted or smoked; and the smell from it, especially when it is being cooked, is very offensive. I could never bring myself to taste any, but a friend of mine who did try it said that it reminded him a little of very green cheese. I came across a group of men at this meal on my way through the village to see the head-man, and they said as I passed, 'Karibu, Bwana, karibu'—'Come, sir, come'— which was equivalent to an invitation to sit down and partake of their food. I nodded to them and smiled, and said, 'Thank you,' as I passed on. An Arab in my place would have accepted the invitation, and sat down and eaten with them; and they would afterwards have spoken of him as their brother when discussing him among themselves, and would have preferred him to the white man, his slave-dealing propensities notwithstanding.

On my return to the tent I found tea ready, a lighter meal than dinner, but somewhat in the same style. This finished, we packed up as many of our goods as we could, in order to leave as little work as possible for the morning; and then began to arrange matters for the night, as rising before four in the morning necessitates retiring to rest very early, especially in a country where more rest is needed than in a temperate climate. At the coast it is often possible to get an hour or two for rest during the hottest part of the afternoon; but on the march, with breakfast after mid-day, this is, of course, out of the question. Our camp-beds were made of canvas tightly stretched across two poles, and supported on three pair of crossed legs; and with a thick rug on the top to take the place of a mattress, were quite comfortable, unless one had fever, when the unyielding canvas became a source of extreme discomfort to one's weary and aching limbs.

The moon was almost overhead now, and we knew that it would set about half-past one in the morning; so we set the alarum for that hour, in order that we might wake and light the lamp before the darkness came on. By always keeping a small light at the entrance to the tent when there was no moon, we were able to have the entire end of the tent open, and enjoy the fresh air, without the disadvantage of being obliged to have men sleeping close in front with their camp-fires alight, and without any danger from wild beasts. As a final precaution, we placed a gun at full-cock across a camp-stool, and then retired to rest. It was best to have the gun so, as the noise produced by cocking it would have injured our chances of a successful shot at any animal that happened to be passing near the tent at night. Sleep soon sealed our weary eyes, and another day's work was over.

CHAPTER VIII

THE SLAVE-TRADE

THE African seems born to be the servant of other nations, and other nations have not been slow to take advantage of this characteristic of his, until much of what sturdy independence he may once have possessed has been crushed out of him, and he seems quite unable now to shake off his indifference to what he considers his inevitable fate.

Yet all Africans are not victims of the slave-trade—at least, of the foreign slave-trade—nor is any particular family entirely under its influence. Amongst the great tribes of the south which belong to the Bantu family, the Zulus, the Kaffirs, the Bechuanas, you do not find the Arab plying his trade; whilst amongst the peoples of the north and north-west many are slaves, although not of the Bantu family. It is where the people are divided up into small tribes of a few thousand souls each that the foreign slave-trade flourishes in all its deadly characteristics. And here let me say at once that there is a great difference—a difference in essence as well as in degree—between the foreign and domestic trade. Domestic slavery is universal throughout Africa, but it is only a kind of feudal system. In each district there is a chief—nominally absolute; really no more absolute than the Czar of Russia. Under him are sub-chiefs, or, more correctly speaking, head-men, whose dependants are their slaves. The sub-chief feeds and protects his man-slave, who works for him, and lives in his house as one of his family. His woman-slave goes to swell the number of his wives, or else becomes the wife of one of his men-slaves. These slaves are obtained through natural increase by birth, by purchase, by capture in time of war, by reception of sick visitors, and of runaways.

Before I went out to Africa, I had, like most people at home, a very simple idea of what slavery was like; so that I was quite unprepared for the complicated system which it really is. Now I understand whence arise those contradictory statements which one hears regarding it, some describing it as a natural beneficial institution, from which its subjects would resent being set free; whilst others go to the other extreme, and denounce it as abhorrent equally in principle as in detail.

Slaves are taken from among the pure or half-caste natives of Africa and its adjacent islands, and only from such as are not subjects of a civilized power. The mere fact of their being Mohammedans does not exempt them from slavery, as some writers have stated. They are obtained now chiefly from the interior, more sparingly from the coast or adjacent territories. Large caravans of Africans who are evidently slaves come down country in charge of Arabs or their native servants; and they are obtained, it is said, chiefly by barter. Caravans of cloth, wire, beads, arms, and ammunition go up country in immense numbers; and on the return journey, slaves and ivory replace these barter goods. Let us trace such an Arab in his journey up country. Newly arrived perhaps from Muscat, he has come to Zanzibar, that El Dorado of Muscat Arabs, there to remain until he has made his fortune and can return home; unless, in the meantime, he contract ties which bind him to his adopted country, a not unlikely event, as it is here that his fellow countrymen rule and fill all the important positions. He has arrived at Zanzibar probably almost penniless; and, consequently, has to engage himself at first as assistant to some brother Arab going up country. For this assistance he receives a little pay, and is able to do a little trading on his own account. He borrows a little money either from his friend or from the Hindus, the great money-lenders and merchants of Zanzibar; and with this purchases sufficient barter goods to buy one or two tusks of ivory, and one or two slaves to carry them. On his return to Zanzibar, if the venture has been successful, he has now a little ready money in hand, perhaps fifty or one hundred pounds, and in addition he has obtained experience as a traveller in the interior. He can now borrow what money he requires from the Hindus; but, of course, at an exorbitant rate of interest. Accordingly he purchases cloth, beads, wire, guns, and ammunition, and either borrows or purchases slaves, obtaining as second in command under himself some Arab still more newly arrived and, consequently, still more needy than himself. He himself and his few trusted head-men will carry breechloaders—if he can afford it, Winchester repeaters—and the remainder of his force ordinary muskets.

Arrived near the scene of his labours, he commences to open negotiations for the supply of slaves he requires. If he knows of any tribe at enmity with its neighbour, he joins himself to the strongest side and assists in an attack on the other, or supports some preposterous claim for damages against the other side; agreeing, however, to compromise for a much smaller sum, he receiving the lion's share of the booty, whether obtained by war or by compromise. I have known an Arab, siding with the chief of one village, go to the chief of another to which the first was hostile, and demand a number of tusks, slaves, etc., on account of a supposed injury done by this second chief to the first; and finally end the quarrel by agreeing to take one good cow, which was probably all that he wanted from the beginning.

In most of the cases which I have come across, the slaves have been purchased by the Arabs from the native chiefs of the interior; and these slaves are stated to be either the scum of the native villages, of whom the chiefs are glad to be rid, or else the prisoners taken by the up-country chiefs in their frequent fights. The natives used to tell me that a smaller trade is done by fraud. Small parties of natives or single individuals are enticed into a caravan to sell food, and are then seized; or else in time of scarcity the people of a half-starved village are encouraged to join themselves to a caravan on the assurance that there is plenty of food a few miles ahead. But the few marches over, the plenty does not make its appearance, and the unfortunate people sadly recognise the fact that they have said farewell to their freedom. Lastly, in time of famine, parents sell their children for food to passing caravans.

These are the principal methods of slave-making that I have come across. In addition, of course, are the organised slave-hunts, where villages are attacked by Arabs or others for the sole purpose of making slaves. These attacks, however, now take place chiefly far in the interior, and of them I know nothing from personal experience. But I doubt if they now form the chief source of supply.

When Tipoo Tib, or as the natives usually call him Tip Tib, passed through Mpwapwa in 1886 with Dr. Jünker, the latter told me that the whole caravan seemed to be composed of slaves, mostly boys. But great chiefs like Tip Tib own large tracts of country, and when they make their pilgrimages to the coast, take with them as slaves apparently whomever they choose to select. Tip Tib told us that he was very anxious to go to relieve Emin himself, and wanted to know if we thought that the English Government would give him the task, if he went to London for the purpose. We told him that we thought Mr. Stanley would probably be asked to go; and that if he went to England in November as he suggested, we thought he would be more likely to get bronchitis than a commission from Government. How he joined himself to Mr. Stanley's caravan at Zanzibar, and went with him to the Congo, and thence to his own home in Manyuema, all the world now knows. I am afraid Tip Tib never got over Mr. Stanley being preferred to him as leader of the expedition.

Bringing slaves and ivory down together seems to be the best paying trade. A tusk which in Uganda and the districts around can be bought for a Snider rifle and a hundred cartridges, will sell at the coast for from twenty to fifty pounds. The slave carries it, so that there is no cost for porterage; whilst the rifle and cartridges, which together cost thirty shillings in Zanzibar, are no expense to bring up country, as caravan porters are only too glad to carry them for their own protection.

Next to the great trade for the foreign market comes the domestic demand and supply for each district. Sometimes the 'necessary' slaves are bought, but frequently every species of fraud is resorted to. In a passing caravan someone gets ill. He can find a ready welcome in many of the huts near; but when he recovers he is not allowed to continue his journey. 'You have eaten my food,' says his kind host, 'and now you are my man.' There was a family living near a station at which I was living who came there in time of famine; and, whilst they were settling down, were given shelter by another family for a day or two. But they lost one of their children in consequence, seized by the good Samaritan who had housed them for the time. I came across several instances of this kind of thing.

When travellers like these who want a helping hand are not plentiful, then stealing is resorted to; as a rule from a neighbouring village which happens not to be on friendly terms. A number of men from a rather hostile village near Kikombo, where I lived for some months, were once prowling about round the place. They saw the little girl of one of our mission men fetching water; and snatched her up in our very garden and fled. Happily some natives near heard her cry, and gave the alarm. Six of the men on the station made a rush for their guns, and then went off in pursuit; on which the thieves, though many in number, instantly dropped their booty, and made their escape over the mountains behind our house.

In the little attacks which the villagers about there occasionally made on each other, a few prisoners were taken now and then; but they were usually ransomed by their friends. Occasionally, however, the attacking force came from a distance, and then negotiations for ransoming were not so easily carried out, especially as the village attacked might not know where its assailants came from.

One day some Wahumba (a branch of the Masai) from the north of Kikombo, passed across the Ugogo plain, and made an attack on the Wahehe, who live to the south, carrying off amongst others, the wife and child of an Mhehe chief. They might never have been recovered, but that the woman was seized with ophthalmia, which, being neglected, resulted in almost complete blindness. In this state she was driven to Kisokwe, where she was rescued by Mr. Cole, the missionary there; her legs then being raw and bruised from the beatings she had received on account of her frequent stumbling along the road, and the delay this caused to her captors. Her child had been taken from her, but she herself, being useless, was willingly left by the Wahumba with Mr. Cole, on payment of a small sum—a dollar, I think, which they demanded as payment for the trouble of bringing her. A week or two of good feeding, and she soon picked up flesh again, and then we sent messengers to the Mhehe chief, who thereupon sent his sons to fetch her.

The lot of the slave woman is the saddest of all. Sometimes amongst the Wanyamwezi and Wagogo, she becomes the wife, with others, of the man who has bought her; and if she bear him children, is kindly treated. Her lot is then perhaps as happy as if she were free (provided she has not left behind a husband and children)—as free, that is, as an African woman ever is, for nearly every one of them must submit to what Canon Taylor euphemistically calls a 'protector.' But if a slave of the Arabs or other travelling traders, she may be simply a miserable tool, handed on from one man to the other at the caprice of the moment. No wonder a converted native, when he wants to marry honourably, gets a girl, if he can, too young to have been handed about for such purposes. Undesirable as these early marriages are, the alternatives are worse.

From this description the reader will understand to some extent how difficult it is for the individual to regain his liberty, or for wholesale measures to be effectively taken against the trade itself. The British Government, it is true, have cruisers along the East African coast, but only occasionally do we hear of their making a capture; and yet one or two hundred caravans containing slaves must pass through Mpwapwa alone in the course of the year. Slaves they are, though it would be difficult to prove it on the spot. They are seldom in chains, and even when they are, that does not absolutely prove them to be slaves. The Sultan's prisoners in Zanzibar work in the streets in slave-chains; and criminals, prisoners of war, and runaways are sometimes treated in the same way up country. I have even known an Englishman send runaway porters up country in slave-chains; the only way to oblige them to work out the time of which they had defrauded him. One gang of about thirty of these cautiously invested their little savings in files before leaving Zanzibar; and at a village about fifty miles from the coast, the head-man woke up one morning to find that thirty of his men had disappeared, and left him thirty heavy chains to carry as best he could. Three men, who either were honest, or had no files, came on as far as Mpwapwa, where I unlocked them at the head-man's request, the result being that one ran away a few days later with his load of cloth. He was caught again, but the cloth was not recovered. When not in chains, it is practically impossible to tell a slave, except here and

Slave Children 219

there. Their owners call them brothers, and the slaves are afraid or unwilling to deny their relationship.

Sometimes there are numbers of children, wan, half-starved little creatures, with that dull look of uncomplaining hopelessness that betrays their condition better than any words of their own or any denials of their master, who will describe them as 'my children,' or by the usual stock phrase, 'the children of my brother.' If you ask the little mites where they come from, they only reply, 'from our home.' Their own names are no help, and as to their father's name, they never knew him as anything else but 'father.'

Another thing that complicates the matter is, that anyone with whom they stay, and who gives them food is called *baba* or *mama* (*i.e.*, father or mother). Sometimes, too, it is their own fathers or mothers who have sold them, so that it would be useless, even if it were possible, to send them back to their homes.

The treatment of children in England by their parents and guardians is sometimes so barbarously cruel, to judge from the Reports of the London Society for the Prevention of Cruelty to Children, that one only wonders that cruel parents are not much more the rule in Central Africa than they actually are. I only occasionally came across cases of cruelty or want of parental affection. A boy was left with me by his parents on their way down country, as he was just recovering from small-pox, and had that day had his ankle crushed by a hyena bite. They seemed to take no interest in him; just leaving him, and not even inquiring about him afterwards. I asked the natives what his parents would have done had he been bitten by the hyena some marches from the mission instead of close to it. 'They would have thrown him away,' was the reply. Yet the children who are sold are few; the stolen many in number. Most of the women on the stations where I was had their stories of children stolen from them, and never seen again.

Some slaves who are left sick on the road do regain their liberty, but as a rule, when so left, they are seized by the one who takes care of them; whilst in many caravans they are not allowed to be sick on the road; it would set a bad example.

When I first came up country an Arab caravan of slaves passed us at Mamboya, going coastward. Stokes, a British trader, who was some days behind us, came upon one of their castaways, a poor old woman. She was too ill to go further, so her

ARAB KILLING A WORN-OUT SLAVE.

master had left her on the road, but had cut her throat first as a warning to the others.

On another occasion a Swahili trader coming down country, after having severely beaten an old woman, who was lagging behind on the march, flung her down and broke her wrist, leaving her to die on the road, but she managed to crawl up to the mission-house. However, no one could speak her language (she was an Mmangati), and though it was easy to heal her sores and feed her up, she could not be persuaded to keep a splint on her arm, so that she soon turned a simple into a compound fracture, and died a day after amputation had been tried, as a last resource.

After slaves have arrived at their destination, or when they are left sick at a mission station, one would expect many of them to try to regain their freedom. But this is only occasionally the case, for they say truly that they have nowhere to run to, and that if they are not the slaves of their present owners, they must be of someone else. The Arabs often used to bring sick slaves to me, and I always agreed to take care of them, but refused to have anything to do with preventing them from regaining their freedom if they wished to make the attempt. Yet of all those who were ever left with me, only one ran away. She was a woman ill with pleurisy. I cured her of her pleurisy, and fed her up, upon which she demanded a house to herself (she was sharing one with another Swahili) and more food, though she was having the usual allowance for convalescents. Some Swahili men enticed her away with the promise of more food, and she disappeared with them.

Hard as is the slave's lot, it is satisfactory to know that the Arab slave-dealer's existence is not all sunshine. Enormous are the profits that during one journey may make their way into his pocket; but the Hindu's fingers are on them if ever he reaches his home. Many, perhaps most, of these Arab traders are deeply in debt to the Hindus of Zanzibar, who are credited with lending them money at a very heavy interest. The Arab, who has the weariness of the long inland journey, comes back laden with his treasures of black and white ivory, only to be fleeced by his stay-at-home Hindu creditor. 'The Arabs are bad enough,' said a German trader to me one day; 'but the Hindus are regular bloodsuckers.'

When a slave caravan has arrived at the coast, the next difficulty is to get it shipped to Zanzibar or elsewhere. The one or two vessels employed by the

Embarkation of Slaves

British Government for the suppression of slavery have to be avoided. If this blockade is not strict, as it rarely can be, the Arab will wait until the position of the blockading vessel and its boats is convenient for his purpose, and the wind favours him, as it does for months together, the monsoons blowing with the utmost regularity, and then he will go where he lists. Or else he will keep his slaves at the coast port until they can speak the language —Swahili; and then ship them openly in detachments, describing them as natives of Zanzibar returning from the mainland. Dhows with fruit and vegetables daily leave the mainland ports for Zanzibar, and half a dozen to a dozen slaves can easily be sent each trip 'to help navigate the vessel.' Occasionally rather too many will be sent, and a few of these overcrowded dhows will perhaps be captured; but the captures are not sufficient in number to deter the slavers in the slightest, nor are they even enough to materially affect the value of the slaves successfully run, the price of a slave being about the same in Zanzibar to-day as it was twenty years ago, although the demand is said to have increased.

The larger number of slaves, however, are run to Pemba, not to Zanzibar, and from there sent elsewhere when the wind and the British gun-boats are both in the right direction.

What becomes of all the slaves that are annually sent down country? How many do come down it is impossible to estimate, so secretly are the coast arrangements transacted, and so few white men are there in the interior to notice the rather more open proceedings which occur there. Yet one can form a rough estimate perhaps from what used to be observable at Mpwapwa, at any rate before it passed into the hands of the Germans two years ago. Mpwapwa is a kind of East Central African 'Clapham Junction.' To it caravan routes from different portions of the interior converge, and from it they diverge again to the various ports on the East coast. Possibly one quarter of the slaves come from Tanganyika and Victoria Nyanza. During twelve months of the time that I was stationed there, I should think two hundred caravans containing varying numbers of slaves must have passed through, going coastward: possibly thirty thousand in all. If this is correct, though it is but a guess, the output of slaves on the East coast alone is not likely to be less than a hundred thousand a year. What becomes of this great multitude? Great numbers are required for the Sultan's towns along

The Foreign Slave Markets

the coast which are held by Arabs, and where slave labour alone is employed. Then comes Zanzibar, with its thousands of Arabs all possessing household slaves. Almost every native in Zanzibar is a slave, even the so-called *wangwana* or 'freemen'; all perform household duties or till the fields and farms. Next comes Pemba, which supplies the world with cloves, all raised by slave-labour, and lastly comes Muscat, the home of the Zanzibar Arab, from which slaves once imported can be exported by land or by coasting dhow, with no one to gainsay, to Arabia, Egypt, Persia, Syria and Turkey.

How can the trade be stopped is a question asked by many now, and asked in real earnest. A glance at the appended map, with some of the chief slave routes indicated, will show that it is not a question of East African policy alone. A blockade, even if effectual, would need to extend three-quarters round Africa, if it were intended to effect something more than diverting and so lengthening most of the routes, and thus merely diminishing the traffic. And the blockade never has been effectual except on the East African coast, and there only during the first half of 1889, when Germany and England between them managed it at an enormous expense. The blockade on the West in the early part of the century did not stop the traffic on that coast; it only ceased when England took possession of the coast itself. Even taking possession of a part of the East

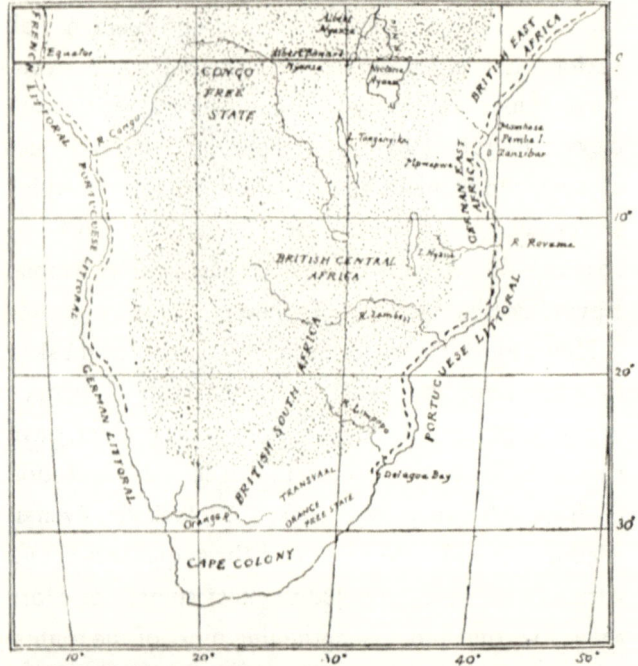

The shaded area is the region of slave-hunting. The interrupted line near the coast shows where slave caravans have been embarked as late as 1889.

coast, as we are doing, and thus preventing the embarkation of slaves from its ports, will again only divert the routes, as it did in West Africa; but of course this diversion, with its consequent lengthening of the route, will render the traffic more expensive, and so diminish, though not stop it. But indirectly, by cutting off the Zanzibar Arab from his supplies, this occupation of the coast will still further hinder the traffic between it and the great lakes. To effect all this, the European rule on the coast must be *real* at each seaport and each seaside village, and such probably will be the case in a very few years; though the effect will be partially neutralised by the increased use of the longer alternative routes, which the Arabs will still have through the Portuguese littoral from Ibo to Delagoa Bay, or through the still more distant outlets north and west.

A year or two ago Commander Cameron proposed to establish a cordon of police up Nyassa, across the country between that lake and the south end of Tanganyika, thence up Tanganyika to the Victoria Nyanza and Albert Edward Nyanza. Such a cordon by itself, however, it is obvious, would act on the traffic routes only as the upheaval of land would do on the river system of any district. It would alter some of their courses, and abolish none of them. But, indirectly, by trading with the native tribes, by being a source of safety to all within reasonable distance, and by giving their countenance to all peaceful undertakings, the agents of Commander Cameron's system, if traders as well as policemen, would gradually teach the native chiefs that it is more profitable to encourage men to work than to sell them. This would help to tap the streams at their fountain-head, and use the victims of slavery for other purposes. With such a cordon, but of traders rather than of police, and the coast-line in the hands of Italian, English, and Germans, the Eastern equatorial slave-trade would practically be abolished. But there would still remain the trade-routes from the centre of Africa to Morocco, to the Egyptian Soudan, and to the Portuguese coast on the west between the Congo and the German colony. The Portuguese coast between Ibo and Delagoa on the east, though still open to the slave-trade, owing to the extremely small number of Portuguese officials available for preventive work, would be of little use for that purpose, as the back-country from Natal to Nyassa will soon be in the hands of the British.

All these methods will be a work of time, and nothing but the abolition of the status of slavery will put a stop at all quickly to the East African trade. But now that the islands of Zanzibar and Pemba, and the northern part of the east coast, have come under British protection, and the southern under German, this abolition, for which Sir Charles Euan-Smith, her Majesty's Agent and Consul-General at Zanzibar, has for the last few years worked so persistently, and which he has already partially obtained, promises before long to be a completely-accomplished fact. Once abolish the status of slavery in these parts, and make the slave free on entering these regions, and you abolish his value to the slave-owner. Nothing will induce an Arab to waste time, money, health, and, perhaps, life, in securing a number of slaves over whom he would have no legal control at the coast, even if he ever succeeded in bringing them there through all the new and added dangers of the way.

But in looking forward to the realization, erelong in its entirety, of Sir Charles Euan-Smith's scheme, we must not forget that, beneficial as the results of that scheme must be to Eastern Equatorial Africa, there will still exist outlets for the slave-trade in the Eastern Soudan and Morocco by which the Arab can still enter the country to devastate it or leave it with his ill-gotten spoil.

The real obstacle to the abolition of the slave-trade lies, of course, in the natives themselves. As long as the natives are split up into small communities of two or three thousand each, so long will they be a prey to any unscrupulous leader of even a small well-armed caravan; and as long as they are eager to sell each other for foreign produce, so long will the slave-dealer find a supply always ready to his hand. Let us hope that the time is not far distant when strong civilized Governments will hold the reins of authority from north to south, and from sea to sea.

'But what right have we,' some people say, 'to go in and take the country from the natives?' This sounds a plausible objection; but Central Africa, we must remember, belongs practically to the Arab slave-hunters. They hold it as an Englishman holds his estate well stocked with game. His game live a wild life, and own no allegiance to him; but they are his, none the less, to spare or to kill, to catch or to loose, when so it pleases him, or when opportunity favours. In this way, then, and for this purpose, the Arab holds Central Africa; and it is from the slave-hunters amongst the Arabs, and not from the natives, that we wrest the authority. We dispossess no chief, subvert no humane laws, take no foot of occupied land; but replace the cruel power and overlordship of the slave-hunter by the fostering care and gentle control of a firm but tender government which gives equal rights to all its subjects, and protects the weaker from the tyranny of the stronger. The only fear is lest any European Government should replace the slavery of the Arab by the far worse slavery of *drink*. However well drinking in moderation may answer amongst the hardy northern peoples of a temperate climate like ours, such moderation is unknown amongst the child-like vacillating races of Central Africa. The Governments which are now stepping in to protect them from the slavery of the Arab, to which they themselves have given every encouragement, must just as firmly protect them from the slavery of drink, which, unfortunately, they are also sure to help on if it once commences. To supply natives with drink would no doubt at the first onset be a distinct advantage—it would create in them a desire for something to obtain which they would need to work; but the temporary advantage would be followed by the ruin of people and country.

To induce natives to work, to give them higher ideas than simply to live from hand to mouth, with no provision for old age, sickness, or even the inevitable occasional local famines, and to do so without the suicidal assistance of drink, is a problem which will tax the best endeavours of our politicians.

But with Sir Francis de Winton's knowledge of the natives, and his tact in dealing with them, and with such a practical philanthropic body as the directors of the Imperial British East Africa Company to encourage him in the work and further his endeavours, the problem, in the British district at any rate, will, I believe, be solved before the rapidly-closing century draws to its end.

CHAPTER IX

THE SLAVE

VERY varied are the descriptions of the slave which we get from different classes of people. In America, the Southerner and Northerner; in Africa, the Arab and native; in Europe, the Englishman and Turk would give very different accounts if asked to describe a slave, and to some extent these different accounts might all be true. The slave can no more be described in one word than the prisoner or the patient; various are the causes which brought him to his present condition, various his characteristics. A slave caravan as it reaches the coast is truly a mixed assembly. In it we find the innocent but unhappy occupier of the soil, torn from wife and home through some native intestine quarrel in which he had taken no part, and the far more unhappy mother whose children have been seized with her, the younger to be ruthlessly thrown into the flames which destroyed her dwelling, the elder to be carried into slavery like herself, and if they survive the dreadful hardships of the march, to be separated from her for ever at the coast, if they have not been lost to her earlier by transfer on the road to some other trader or some other caravan, as is not infrequently the case. But accompanying these deserving objects of pity, and forming no inconsiderable portion of the entire caravan are the loafers and idlers of many an interior village, whose chiefs keep no workhouse and levy no rates for tramps, but who rid themselves of their drones in a summary and profitable way; and lastly the criminal classes, who under more civilized Governments would be occupying the prisons at the public expense, and who under the Arabs would be working in the fields in chains, have under the less civilized rule of Central Africa been turned to more profitable account and sent to swell the property of the passing Arab, whose cloth and powder, in return, has gone to enrich their quondam chief.

A man who has been a domestic slave up country, and who has been transferred to the coast, the hardships of the march once over, is not necessarily in a worse condition than he was in before, provided he is not sent to a foreign country. He was a domestic slave before, and when he settles down in his new master's home on the coast, provided that master be an Arab, as he probably will be, he practically becomes a domestic slave again. His fellow-slaves and his overseers are Africans like himself; his Arab master even has much in common with him, and does not disdain to eat with him, or to be on friendly terms with him.

But a slave is, of course, the absolute property of his master; and though that does not necessitate his being ill-treated, it gives him no guarantee of good treatment, and it takes away all rights from him, all responsibility. He may perhaps marry, but at any moment he may have his children taken from him, or sold elsewhere, or his wife sent away. He may be beaten, tortured, or even killed, provided it is done quietly enough, if on the coast, or under an excuse of witchcraft, if in the interior. A slave is not necessarily a man ill-treated, but he is a man without rights. He has no law to protect him, no creature to whom he can appeal. Men say: 'Oh, self-interest makes men look after their slaves;' but it is not always so, and as Mr. Hay Aitken has well put it,* ' How little do considerations of reasonable self-interest weigh with those who are under the influence

* 'Eastertide.' By W. Hay M. H. Aitken, M.A. London: John F. Shaw and Co.

of a single besetting sin! We lean upon a broken reed when we trust to the principles of the utilitarian to save men from their follies and their crimes. It is, as the writer of the Epistle to the Hebrews says, the heart is " hardened by the *deceitfulness* of sin." '

Consequently, slaves do occasionally run away from their masters, though usually only when the master is cruel, and when the slave knows of some place to which he can go with a reasonable chance of escaping recapture. Such places of refuge some of the mission stations in East Africa have been. One small station, Fulladoyo, was so crowded with slaves that the missions, I believe, withdrew from it to avoid complications with the Arabs. But the runaways there were, even then, quite in sufficient numbers to protect themselves from Arab attacks, and their numbers have steadily increased to several thousand by additions from the households of cruel Arab masters, and also, until the danger was discovered by the Arabs and the route changed, by runaways from passing caravans. These Fulladoyo people are quiet and peace-abiding, enjoying the sweets of freedom, but unable to come to the coast or leave their district for fear of recapture.

The existence of such a colony is a proof that the life of even a domestic slave at the coast is not all honey, as some would have us believe; but at the same time, the presence of so many hundreds of slaves within one day's march of it, and of many thousands within easy access, shows that escape from slavery is not considered much of a prize by the majority of slaves, and that the greater proportion of Arab masters are evidently not brutal to their bond-servants.

The condition of insecurity under which the slave exists often begets in him the most extreme apathy. Not infrequently, his one idea is to escape work, to get food and ease by lying, thieving, cheating; in fact, by anything except hard work. And it is this very condition of the slave's morals, that is, of the slave who has been brought up as such from childhood or youth, as most have, which makes the whole question of freeing the slave such an exceedingly complicated one to deal with. There is an enormous population of irresponsible idlers; from youth upwards they have been trained in the paths of idleness and vice, and as a man sows, so shall he reap. Slave-owners in the past, no doubt, are responsible for the present degraded condition of the African slave; but that does not alter the fact that, in working for them, we are face to face with a degraded people, who all their life long have sown to the flesh, and now are reaping to the flesh. Indeed, most of them have no desire to escape from slavery; by it they get food and clothing and a provision in old age, with only occasionally excessively hard work. If they lose their wives by sale, they may get others instead; and in picturing to ourselves the harrowing scene of a husband and wife being separated, we are apt to forget that one word—polygamy, included in the description of such an occurrence, will give it another aspect, and explain the statement which is often made, and sometimes with truth, that their feelings and ours under such separations may be really very different. It is not the slave-owners, but the slaves, who will be the difficult problem in the civilization of Africa.

Face to face with the man brought up in slavery, you realize that childhood is the time of sowing and manhood the time of reaping, and that you cannot reap in manhood what you have not sown in childhood; you cannot even get them to desire the freedom which we look upon as such a precious birthright. Slaves from Zanzibar come up country in the caravans in large numbers, and travel into the interior of the continent; yet almost invariably return to their masters when their work is done, although there would be no one to stop them if they chose to run away. Even when dissatisfied with their condition, they are not anxious to change it, it might be, for the worse. Amongst the unmarried, this is intelligible; but amongst the married even, who for the sake of their families ought to desire freedom, slavery breeds the same painful apathy. When I was in the interior, I knew natives on the mission stations who were runaway slaves—couples, some who were joined in wedlock after coming to us; yet in many, indeed, by far the most instances, the husbands had not saved up enough money to buy either their own freedom or that of their wives. Their former owner, or one of his many 'brothers,' used to make his appearance in the neighbourhood; for a moment there was a scare amongst these people, and they used to talk about measures for securing their freedom. Presently the cause of their alarm, not being aware of their proximity, went his way, and all subsided into their usual apathy. Some of these natives had been on the mission stations for years without taking any steps against recapture, and yet two years' careful husbanding of wages on the part of any one of them would easily have purchased the freedom of both himself and his wife. To many a slave have I given work and urged him to labour until he had saved enough money for this purpose; yet, though he knew that at any moment he and his wife might be claimed, and perhaps sold to different masters, and so separated, I only succeeded in getting one man to persevere.

Slaves are creatures of to-day, with no thought for the morrow. As General Gordon so tersely put it: 'The bird in the hand is worth any number in the bush. It is useless to argue with them; they are deaf to it. They have got the bird, and mean to keep him; in words they are fatalists, in acts they are the reverse.' They have no desire to be pure or truthful or honest or independent. They love sin, and do not want separation from it. They love the possible idleness of slavery, even with all its other possibilities of cruel work and barbarous treatment. They must be taught to hate sin, before they can be taught to hate slavery. It is all very well to rescue Oliver Twist from Fagin's den. You can do it, because he already hates the life; but you cannot rescue the others; they will only go back to it. They have sown to the flesh. 'Not their own fault,' you say. True. But they must reap, all the same. One sometimes hears boys in England trying to extenuate their sins by saying: 'Others are more to blame than I; I was taught this sin by others who were older and knew better than I did what they were doing.' True; but they will have to reap what they have sown none the less, however much more others may be to blame than themselves. Many will help or encourage a fellow to sow his wild oats; but how many will lend a hand when the inevitable reaping comes. It would give many an English boy a help upwards in fighting temptation if he could come out to Africa and see the almost hopeless state of those who live out their boyhood in sin, even though it is far less their own fault than that of others who encouraged them in the downward path.

Many of these adult slaves when freed are handed over to us by Government. But what can be done for them? Very little. Not many of them are willing to do steady honest work; and some, I fear many, go voluntarily back into slavery again. They prefer their Arab masters to their English or German deliverers, who want them to work hard, and who do not treat them as if they were fellow-countrymen. Their Arab masters, if already possessed of many slaves, do not require much work from them; and though they will kick them one day, will sit down to a meal with them on the next, and behave as their brother or father. There is a good deal of human nature in such a preference. People of any colour prefer those who treat them as brothers to those who treat them as servants only, even though the brother may be hasty and bad-tempered, and the master just and good-tempered.

The two great incentives to work amongst these peoples of Central Africa, whether slaves or not, appear to be the fear of hunger and the fear of punishment. But neither of these causes contributes to any prolonged foresight on their part. As Mr. Herbert Spencer says, when speaking of the lowest tribes, 'A year is the longest period to which their conduct is adapted. Hardly yet worthy to be defined as creatures "looking before and after," they show by their utter improvidence, and their apparent incapacity to realize future consequences, that it is only to the conspicuous and oft-recurring phenomena of the seasons that their actions respond.' But that they are not incapable of a higher degree of foresight than they now possess, seems evident, both from the much higher state to which the Waganda have attained, and from the customs amongst others of the natives living upon and behind the Portuguese coast, who although not semi-civilized like the Waganda, yet are in the habit of coming through Zululand to Natal and there working for three or four years, until they have accumulated sufficient to purchase a wife and small homestead, when they will return with their wealth, this time by sea to avoid the Zulus, and settle down in their own country. Many of the Wanyamwezi, too, have as frugal habits; but generally speaking, the majority of the natives and all of the slaves are characterized by a great deficiency in foresight. But the abolition of polygamy, the enforcement of moral laws, obligatory clothing, and the compulsory support of the aged will all tend to discourage idleness and stimulate the desire to labour.

Mr. O'Neill, R.N., our late Consul at Mozambique, in his thorough and practical little pamphlet on the 'Nyassa Slave Trade' (1885), says, when treating of the question which we have been considering, that it is from the native artisans taught by the British that he looks for the most useful results, 'by the example they set to those of their own colour of social superiority, of skilled industry and steady labour. It is by showing the native in this practical manner what he is capable of, and creating in him a desire to go and do likewise, that he is drawn insensibly into those habits which impress most deeply and beneficially his character, and do more than all else towards his regeneration and civilization.' I wish I could feel as confident on this subject as Mr. O'Neill; but I fear that a weak point in the argument lies in the sentence, 'And creating in him a desire to go and do likewise.' Except for the very exceptional Central African, I doubt much if such a desire will be created by merely 'showing him what he is capable of.' He is far too satisfied with his own condition and his own way of doing things. But the younger generation who will be brought up to reverence their fathers' masters more than their fathers, and who from their earliest years will now see the far-reaching advantages of labour, especially of skilled labour, and who will not grow up under the disadvantage of having their ideas stereotyped before being brought in contact with the white man, will, I believe, reap the harvest which one would fain see the present African enjoy.

It seems evident, therefore, that our chief object should be not so much to free those who have been brought up in slavery as to free the children, and, by preventing more captures, stop the further wholesale degradation of the African who is capable of so much better things.

As regards the adults, Mr. George Mackenzie's plan seems the only feasible one—viz., to give every adult slave an opportunity of working out his own freedom, and to grant to any man or woman their freedom on these conditions, and these conditions only. Six months' hard work under existing circumstances will easily effect this. But the youths and the children—poor little mites!—surely some means can be adopted to free them before it is too late, and they become demoralized like their elders. Some measures towards this end have already been put into force by Sir Charles Euan-Smith, whose philanthropic energy and foresight obtained them from Seyyid Khalifa, the present Sultan's predecessor on the throne; and obtained them with surprisingly little opposition from the slaveholders, for the esteem and regard in which he is held by Arab and European alike enabled him to satisfy conflicting claims without the disheartening delays which would have been experienced by those who, unlike him, were not in such complete possession of the confidence and affection of the Arab.

The experience of the past gives us every right to expect that such measures as these would result in the greatest good to the country; for it is from amongst the child-slaves of Africa, rescued by British men-of-war, and handed over to our missions, that almost all the true and reliable Christians of East Africa have been recruited.

Note.—One of the last acts of Sir Charles Euan-Smith before leaving Zanzibar was to obtain from the Sultan the sweeping reforms in the slave-traffic included under the following decree:

IN THE NAME OF GOD, THE MERCIFUL, THE COMPASSIONATE.

THE FOLLOWING DECREE IS PUBLISHED BY US,

SEYYID ALI BIN SAID,

SULTAN OF ZANZIBAR, AND IS TO BE MADE KNOWN TO, AND TO BE OBEYED BY, ALL OUR SUBJECTS WITHIN OUR DOMINIONS FROM THIS DATE.

DECREE

1. We hereby confirm all former decrees and ordinances made by Our Predecessors against Slavery and the Slave Trade and declare that whether such decrees have hitherto been put in force or not, they shall for the future be binding on Ourselves and on Our Subjects.
2. We declare that, subject to the conditions stated below, all Slaves lawfully possessed on this date by our Subjects, shall remain with their owners as at present. Their status shall be unchanged.
3. We absolutely prohibit, from this date, all exchange, sale, or purchase of Slaves, domestic or otherwise. There shall be no more traffic whatever in Slaves of any description. Any houses, heretofore kept for traffic in domestic Slaves by Slave Brokers, shall be for ever closed, and any person found acting as a Broker for the exchange or sale of Slaves, shall be liable, under Our orders, to severe punishment, and to be deported from Our dominions. Any Arab, or other of Our Subjects, hereafter found exchanging, purchasing, obtaining, or selling domestic or other Slaves, shall be

liable under Our orders to severe punishment, to deportation, and the forfeiture of all his Slaves. Any house in which traffic of any kind in any description of Slave may take place shall be forfeited.

4. Slaves may be inherited at the death of their owner only by the lawful children of the deceased. If the owner leaves no such children, his Slaves shall *ipso facto* become free on the death of their owner.

5. Any Arab, or other of Our Subjects, who shall habitually ill-treat his Slaves, or shall be found in the possession of raw Slaves, shall be liable under Our orders to severe punishment, and, in flagrant cases of cruelty, to the forfeiture of all his Slaves.

6. Such of Our Subjects as may marry persons subject to British Jurisdiction, as well as the issue of all such marriages, are hereby disabled from holding Slaves, and all Slaves of such of Our Subjects as are already so married are now declared to be free.

7. All Our Subjects who, once Slaves, have been freed by British Authority, or who have long since been freed by persons subject to British Jurisdiction, are hereby disabled from holding Slaves, and all Slaves of such persons are now declared to be free.

All Slaves who, after the date of this decree may lawfully obtain their freedom, are for ever disqualified from holding Slaves, under pain of severe punishment.

8. Every Slave shall be entitled, as a right, at any time henceforth, to purchase his freedom at a just and reasonable tariff to be fixed by Ourselves and Our Arab Subjects. The purchase money on Our order shall be paid by the Slave to his owner before a Kadi, who shall at once furnish the Slave with a paper of freedom, and such freed Slaves shall receive Our special protection against ill-treatment. This protection shall also be specially extended to all Slaves who may gain their freedom under any of the Provisions of this Decree.

9. From the date of this Decree, every Slave shall have the same rights as any of Our other Subjects who are not Slaves, to bring and prosecute any complaints or claims before Our Kadis.

Given under Our Hand and Seal this 15th day of El Hej, 1307, at Zanzibar.
(August 1st, A.D. 1890.)

[*Signed*]
ALI BIN SAID,
Sultan of Zanzibar.

(Seal.)

CHAPTER X

THE ARAB

THE Arab, like the slave, is very variously described by different writers. In the opinion of some, his adherence to Mohammedanism and his brave warlike nature place him on an eminence as high as, if not higher than, that of the Christian; whilst to others, he is the incarnation of all that is brutal and devilish—the homeless man, whose fate it is to break up homes wherever he finds them; the sensual profligate, whose name, turned into an adjective, is used to designate the lowest forms of immorality.

It is less than eighty years since the Arabs from Oman in Arabia, sailing southward in their swarm of dhows and English-built frigates, threw themselves upon the East African coast and adjacent islands, and dispossessed the effete Portuguese. The Portuguese had held those regions at intervals ever since Vasco da Gama rounded the Cape of

Good Hope—or, as he called it, the Cape of Storms—and, sailing northwards, unfurled the flag of his country over districts which had never before known civilization—never, that is, if we may except the very hypothetical visit of the sailors of Solomon, who perhaps came in a bygone age to barter the produce of Syria and Egypt for the gold of Africa.

Zanzibar once taken by the Arabs was soon used as the base from which expeditions, chiefly for the purchase and capture of slaves, were made into the far interior. From it the Arab set out on his long and often perilous journey with cloth, guns, and ammunition; and to it he returned with his usually ill-gotten gains of slaves and ivory, and no doubt with some fairly-gotten produce from the lands which give birth to the Nile and the Congo. His journey was not only a march of brutal force; he bartered honestly with many tribes through whose districts he passed, and so opened up trade-routes which but for him would even now have been impassable for the missionary and the explorer. He did more than this in his unintentional assistance to civilization; he taught his adopted language, Swahili, to some amongst all the tribes with whom he came in contact, until he had made it the trade-language of more than half of Central Africa, and so paved the way for the rapid diffusion of Gospel knowledge by the missionary who followed in his track. The Arab has done for Africa what the Romans did for Europe when they gave it one great language for commercial use—a partial unity of tongue, without which Christianity could never have overspread our Continent with one-half the rapidity with which it actually did.

Dignified courtesy, courage, and perseverance are the better characteristics of the Arab, whose evil qualities, however, when he is known at home, do certainly rather neutralize his good ones, though unnecessary cruelty and disregard for the feelings of others is not, so far as I know, by any means a predominant feature in his character, as many writers on the slave-trade assert. He does not, as a rule, ill-treat his slaves, and they usually prefer him to even an English or a German master. Even the worst of the race—the slave-hunting Arab (for all Arabs are not slave-hunters)—is not always intentionally brutal to his victims. The Arab, like the Englishman of even the last century, looks upon the African as specially constructed to be his servant. He knows he is to be obtained best and cheapest in the far interior; so thither he wends his way, and, by fair means and foul, collects together a vast herd of victims. Now begin the dreadful horrors of the march; but they are horrors which necessarily accompany a march commenced under such circumstances, and are not superadded by the intentional brutality of the Arab. Directly one unfortunate slave is seized with illness and unable to continue the journey, he is, as a rule, if the caravan is still near the hunting-ground, killed by the Arab in charge. If this custom were not the rule, the whole caravan would get ill at the next station, and cry out that it was quite impossible for them to proceed. If it is necessary to transport a body of slaves from the interior to the coast, then the only plan is to kill those too ill to travel. This sounds rather a cold-blooded statement; but I think the reader will see on reflection that it is correct. The system of slavery is diabolical. You cannot carry it out on *couleur de rose* principles; and an Arab, or an Englishman of the Elizabethan age of which we are so proud, who so far forgot his duty to his neighbour as to assist in it, was dragged by force of circumstances into committing horrible cruelties which the best-intentioned, kindest-hearted man could no more avoid than the most brutal one. We must abolish slavery, and by God's help we will; but it is not our duty to abolish the Arab, or, as one traveller and philanthropist has said, 'Wipe every Arab off the face of Africa.'

At Zanzibar and on the adjacent mainland, an Arab Sultan rules and levies taxes, and Arab nobles under him hold the reins of government and nominally own the country. Nominally I say, because their lands and houses are in most cases so heavily mortgaged to the British Indian subjects, that they and not the Arabs are in most cases the real owners. These ruling Arabs then are the aristocracy of the Zanzibar-Arab nation, and they usually live and die in the country which owns their sway; but there are many others who either are too obnoxious politically to the Sultan to live at all in Zanzibar, or too heavily in debt to the Banyans to live in comfort there, and these usually penetrate into the interior, and there remain until either they have redeemed their ruined fortunes, or until a new Sultan shall arise, who knows neither them nor their offences. Meanwhile they live in comfort in one of the Arab settlements few and far between, where, safe from the wrath of their Sultan, who cannot, or from the attentions of the Banyans who dare not, penetrate into the interior, they live lives of moderate comfort; exiles, but with the companionship of fellow-countrymen, and in the enjoyment of the sweets of liberty. Although, perhaps, a considerable proportion of those who make Central Africa their home are the riff-raff of the Arab nation, and largely responsible for the ill odour in which the Arab is held in the interior, yet whenever you come across him, whether at the coast, or in the remotest deserts, you usually find in him the same courteous manners and the same readiness to entertain strangers with his always polite, somewhat superficial, but none the less agreeable, hospitality. The Englishman who has troubled himself little about manners in his own country, will find himself much at a disadvantage in dealing with the polished, dignified Arab, even in the wilds of Central Africa.

These Arab settlements, of which we have spoken, sparsely scattered over the interior, inhabited by but few Arabs with their retainers, powerful only by comparison with the utter feebleness of the native 'powers' around, are nevertheless useful as bases of operation and cities of refuge for the slave-hunters during their expeditions into the interior. One would naturally have supposed that the mission stations would have been antagonistic to these Arab settlements, and the missionaries obnoxious to the Arabs. But this is by no means the case. The missionary has no power to release the slaves in the Arab caravans or settlements, and even if he had the power to release those who desired freedom, he would be quite unable to feed them after their release. The Arab and the slave both know this, and consequently desertions of slaves to the mission stations, except at the coast, are few and far between. Far from objecting to them, the Arabs find the mission stations a great convenience on their expeditions. Often an Arab on his journey would come to me and ask for some few necessaries in the way of supplies, with which I was usually able to furnish him; or a sick Arab would come for medicine, or for medical comforts such as arrowroot or biscuits; or a wounded one would come for surgical dressings to take with him on his journey. Then, too, an Arab who had sick slaves in his caravan, instead of killing them as a warning to the others, would bring them to the mission and leave them there. I have had many handed over to me in this way, and I always willingly took care of them, only stipulating that I should be allowed to let them run away before their master came back; to which their master willingly assented, knowing well that there was no place to which they could escape, and only laughingly suggesting that, on my part, I should promise not to sell them to anyone else myself. On other occasions, an Arab, with a heavy cargo of ivory, finding the number of his slave-carriers so diminished by desertions or death, that he could not convey his treasures to the coast, would gladly take the opportunity of leaving at some mission station the surplus which he could not carry. In this way I have sometimes had some three or four thousand pounds worth of ivory in the cellar of my house, left there by some passing Arab with no other assurance than a verbal promise that I would look after it for him. Such confidence have Arabs in the English missionaries, that I have before now, far in the interior, paid them for goods with an English cheque which they at once accepted at the value which I told them it represented. Mr. Ashe, in his 'Two Kings of Uganda,' gives a similar instance of their confidence: 'After two or three days' journey through the scrubby forest, we came on an Arab caravan going to Unyanyembe. The Arabs visited me, and I told them I wanted to buy a donkey which they had with them. The owner of the donkey had only lately come from Muscat, and did not know whether a bill from me was worth having. However, his friend assured him that I was an Englishman, and that it would be all right. So in an African wilderness, five hundred miles from Zanzibar, this stranger

His Trust in Englishmen 257

Arab handed over to me a fine Muscat donkey, with saddle and trappings, in exchange for a dirty piece of paper, with an order written in English for one hundred and ten dollars. It was a heavy price, but I seldom, I think, have made a better bargain than the splendid little animal, which proved a godsend to me on my journey. I have mentioned this incident, as I think it shows that Englishmen had gained credit from the Arabs for being, at any rate, honourable in their dealings.'

The Arabs have not been unmindful of the assistance which they have at various times received from missionaries in the interior. Even when the anti-European feeling was at its highest, just after the bombardment of the East African coast towns by the German men-of-war, only one Arab governor sent orders up country to kill the English in the interior, and even he relented under pressure from the Sultan, and let the first band of four (Mr. Ashe, my wife and child and myself) safely through his district, though shortly afterwards he murdered a friend of ours, who came down to the coast by the same route. He was the only Englishman killed during the war.

Although the Arabs, like other Mohammedans, fiercely resent one of their number becoming a

Christian, they are not on that account hostile to Christians, who have not been Mohammedans; nor do they take much, if any trouble, to convert either Christian or heathen to Mohammedanism. The heathen coast man, the converted native from the interior, who has turned from heathenism to Christ *and who has never been a Mohammedan,* the Buddhist from India and the Parsee fire-worshipper, all alike live in peace, and pursue unhindered and unpersecuted their religious observances in the Arab-ruled towns of Zanzibar and the coast. The Arabs will even speak of what they consider the decay of their religion with perfect equanimity, and I have known some even affirm, with the most complete indifference, that when the Turkish Empire is destroyed, Mohammedanism will become a thing of the past. So far as I have been able to gather from my intercourse with them, they do not even object to a missionary speaking to them of the claims of Christ; only they consider any personal questions as to their own individual belief an exhibition of bad manners and want of courtesy on the part of their questioner. Yet there is a religious sect, the Wahabbees (Mohammedan Puritans, Mackay has called them) who, when in power, are certainly very intolerant towards Christianity; but then they are equally intolerant towards Mohammedanism which is not of their exact colour. They are, however, only a sect, and by no means represent the Arab race.

All that I have seen of the Arab in East and Central Africa so completely agrees with the description given of him by Palgrave as he saw him in his native home in Arabia that I cannot do better than quote his remarks: 'It is true that among a very large number, this immense latitude of belief has led to an equally or even a more logical sequence, namely, entire scepticism; and a settled resolution to prefer the certain to the uncertain, the present to the future.

> ' " Shall I abandon the pleasures of the pure wine-goblet
> For all they tell me about milk and honey hereafter;
> Life, and death, and resurrection to follow,
> —Stuff and nonsense, my dear madam,"

are the too celebrated lines of a very popular Arab poet, and I have often heard them quoted in moments of unreserved conversation with unequivocal approval on the part of all present. Not that even thus the Arab exactly disbelieves, but he has made up his mind not to "fash his thumb" about the matter.

'That the Turks are in their way a religious people may be fully admitted. That the Mogols, the inhabitants of Balkh and Bokhara, of Herat and Beloochistan, are even more religious, nationally, and individually, I am entirely convinced. But, at whatever risk of startling my readers accustomed, perhaps, to a popularly opposite view of the case, I must protest against the right of the Arabs as such to be in any way entitled a religious nation. Had the Mohammedan scheme been entrusted to Arab keeping alone; had not Persian, Mogol, Turkish, nay, at times European influence and race come in to its aid, few would have been ere this the readers of the Koran and the fasters of Ramadan.'

As to 'sweeping the Arab off the face of Africa,' or attempting to 'abolish him,' or any other similarly drastic measure, people who suggest such methods can have little idea of what he is really like. The courage of the Arabs in war, their enterprise in times of peace, their affection for one another, their readiness to receive the African almost as an equal, the devotion of the children, and even the slaves, to their father or master makes them a united body far more formidable and powerful than people at home are apt to imagine. But for their religion, which gives them no incentive to fight against the impurity, deceit and cruelty only too inherent in fallen man, whether white or coloured, I doubt if they would fall much behind the Englishmen of the Middle Ages. Again I find that my observations but bear out those of the far more experienced traveller mentioned before, whose words I again quote. 'Some travellers have said that the Persians are the Frenchmen of the East; perhaps they said it in haste, indeed, I hope so, for to compare Europeans with Persians is but a bad compliment to the former. If, however, such-like vague and incomplete comparisons can bear a real meaning, I would unhesitatingly affirm Arabs to be the English of the Oriental world.

'A strong love and a high appreciation of national and personal liberty, a hatred of minute interference and special regulations, a great respect for authority so long as it is decently well exercised, joined with a remarkable freedom from anything like caste-feeling in what concerns ruling families and dynasties; much practical good sense, much love of commercial enterprise, a great readiness to undertake long journeys and voluntary expatriation by land and sea in search of gain and power, patience to endure, and perseverance in the employment of means to ends, courage in war, vigour in peace, and, lastly, the marked predominance of a superior race over whomever they came in contact with among their

Asiatic or African neighbours, a superiority admitted by these last as a matter of course and acknowledged right; all these are features hardly less characteristic of the Englishman than of the Arab; yet that these are features distinctive of the Arab nation, taken, of course, on its more favourable side, will hardly, I think, be denied by any experienced and unprejudiced man. This, I need not say, like most other broad statements, admits of many exceptions.'

The Arab completely released from the curse of Islam, which does more harm by standing in the way of his development than by actually corrupting him, would be a really fine character; and he is so thoroughly fitted, both physically, intellectually, and socially, for work in the interior of Africa, that if he could but be brought to the saving knowledge of Christ, the difficult question of the evangelization of the Dark Continent would practically be solved.

CHAPTER XI

THE MISSIONARY

WITH the material in the previous chapters before the reader, he will be better able to realize the position and work of the missionary, and to get a grasp of the difficulties which he is called upon to encounter, and the problems which present themselves to him to be solved. His aim, I take it, in going to such a place as Africa, is not because he can find no work at home—not because he longs for more exciting, less monotonous methods of doing good than England affords; but simply because he believes that his Master has given the order to His disciples to go out into all the world, and preach the gospel to every creature; not only to tell them of the remission of sins; but also, and this is a much more comprehensive and life-long work, to teach them to observe all things, whatsoever He has commanded; briefly, not only to teach them to work that His Kingdom may come; but also that, in every detail of their daily life, His will may be done. The great enemy we have to contend with in East Africa is indifference; not slavery itself is such a barrier as this, nor even Mohammedanism, great as the obstacle which this system presents in North Africa and India. The Mohammedanism of East Equatorial Africa, so far as my experience goes, is almost entirely confined to Zanzibar, Pemba, and the coast lands. The Arabs and half-Arabs, who are the ruling classes in Zanzibar, are Mohammedans, and so are the upper classes in the large coast towns; but the Swahili of the coast are only nominal Mohammedans, who know little about and care less for the religion which they profess to hold. Except when in Zanzibar, or at the coast towns, I have never seen a Swahili perform any other religious duty than to turn a sheep or goat towards Mecca before he cut its throat. The Swahili, in fact, are heathen; their heathenism being altered partly by Mohammedanism, and in so far as it is altered by this, certainly for the better, but partly also by the semi-civilization of Zanzibar; and it is this civilization, devoid of Christianity, which makes work amongst the coast people so difficult and unsatisfactory.

Their great feature then is an extraordinary in-

The Barrier of Indifference 265

difference to the future—an indifference partly due to the fewness of their wants, which enables them to supply themselves with all they need by one or two hours' work a day; and, partly, to the system of domestic slavery almost universal throughout Africa which, by giving them an absolute master, often prevents them from storing up for the future (for all that they have belongs to their master); and also releases them from the necessity of even thinking of the morrow; for their master, they know, must feed them for fear they should run away. This indifference is not shown to religion only, or even chiefly, but with complete impartiality to religious, social, and personal matters. Whilst this indifference is the great barrier to their acceptance of Christ as their Saviour; their belief in witchcraft is the great obstacle to their trusting His word, and being able to love their neighbours as themselves. But with their general indifference there is much true affection towards their own people, and that is the one great feature in their character which the missionary can work upon. If they learn about Christ, they try to spread the news. I believe a much larger percentage of these converts work amongst their fellow-countrymen than is the case at home. Others, besides myself, have been struck by one of the first acts of native converts when they come to the knowledge of the truth. They pray for their relations who never heard the good news, and died long ago in ignorance. Another good feature is their humility. At once, when they realize what God's commands mean, they frankly admit their inability to comply with them, and grasp at the idea of an indwelling Holy Spirit who shall give them a power which they do not naturally possess.

There is much, therefore, to work upon in these people; and yet the slowness of the process and the result so deferred take away anything like romance from the work, even after the monotonous time spent in learning the language has been passed, and the missionary is actively engaged amongst the people with whom he has come to live. Learning the language is, of course, the first consideration. It is useless to work through interpreters; a native interpreter naturally gives a free translation of what you say, which frequently means a free translation of what you do not say. Again, you can only speak when your interpreter is with you, and so obviously can never speak to a man alone; and a man who is willing to open his heart to you is not always willing to do so to the interpreter. For acquiring Swahili no special aptitude for languages is required, though, of course, it is advantageous. The language is easily learnt by anyone who will take pains and persevere, and who will live much amongst the natives. In learning it, an interpreter is invaluable; and he is especially useful in an indirect way. The learner, if he frequently talks with him in English and notes all his peculiar sentences, will find that he translates literally into English the idioms of his native tongue.

The language once acquired, the missionary is in a position to commence work in earnest amongst the people with whom he comes in contact. He can, of course, devote himself to work amongst children or adults or both; but the work amongst children is really quite distinct from that amongst adults; and I think, as a rule, requires a different type of man to effect it successfully. Wherever the white man goes, there the children will flock to him from sheer curiosity; and if he is kind to them, some will come to be taught to read. But it is usually impossible to get them to come regularly, except by giving them work to do on the station and paying them small but fair wages either in cloth or food or both. Once taught to read, they can be more fully instructed out of the Bible, from which they have in the meantime been taught; and they will learn partly by reading and committing to memory the lessons contained in it, and partly by watching the missionary put them into practice himself. The method of teaching to read is slightly different to that employed in England. Being unable to pronounce a closed syllable like the letter *f*, they are usually taught open syllables at once, instead of letters. Thus:

ba	be	bi	bo	bu
gwa	gwe	gwi	gwo	gwu
mba	mbe	mbi	mbo	mbu
nga	nge	ngi	ngo	ngu.

They have such very retentive memories that they quickly learn the syllables off by heart without, perhaps, having the vaguest idea which symbol stands for which. A boy will often repeat a whole page of syllables without a mistake; but cover part of the page and show him one of the syllables by itself, and he will not have the least idea what it is.

One might briefly describe the boys of Central Africa as being merry, good-natured, affectionate, untruthful, and idle. It is very difficult to get them even to play games with any energy, unless one has them entirely under one's own control, as in the case of freed slave boys handed over to the missions by the Government, or foundlings left on their hands. I suppose this want of energy, which they share with the men, is the natural outcome of the continual enervating heat. Yet the boys are sometimes quite in earnest both in work and play, and as quick as the men in seeing the applicability of God's Word to their own condition. I remember a happy, pleasant-faced boy at Kisokwe named Nzala, who had listened attentively for some days to Mr. Cole, as he was preaching to the elder people there, and who applied to him for baptism. Cole said: 'You are very young, and do not know God's Word sufficiently; I think you had better wait.' But the boy satisfied him that he did understand, and still pressed for baptism; then Cole, who knew the danger of taking boys too quickly at their word, or letting them trust to first impressions, again suggested waiting. 'But,' said Nzala, 'you yourself told us the other day that now is the accepted time, now is the day of salvation.' Finally, he gained his end, and was baptized and became a sincere worker. After some time, he one day lost his temper over some trifling matter, and went straight back into heathenism again, as so many converts do. Prayer was made on his behalf; and after a while, like the prodigal son, he came to himself and returned to the mission station again, a quieter and a humbler boy.

This going back again of the convert into heathenism is very disheartening at first to the missionary. Afterwards it is saddening, but not so disheartening to him when he comes to realize more the difficulties of a convert's position, especially if he be a boy. There are several things which combine to render his position difficult. In the first place the convert, previous to conversion, has never been taught, and never attempted, to restrain any of his passions; and, consequently, they have a fearful hold over him. Then, although God's grace is sufficient for his need as for ours, yet he knows at first almost nothing of the very promises which could help him upward, and which St. Peter tells us are given unto us that by means of them we may become partakers of the Divine nature, having escaped 'the corruption that is in the world through lust.' Again, he has not the same protection that we have in moral surroundings. Always before his eyes are the very sins which he would fain escape; and when he does fall, as Christians in England fall, he naturally, as they, is most prone to fall into the old sins which no public opinion ever taught him to avoid, and for the commission of which no public opinion will blame him. So where an English Christian will fall into selfishness, temper, or pride, the African will fall into theft, open immorality, or violence. Lastly, and this is a very important factor in judging the native convert, his life is all before the public. There are no doors inside his house; no rooms into which he can shut himself. All he does is known to all the world. When we do particularly sinful actions, it is usually within closed doors; and the world never knows, and the Church never guesses, and the critic continues to think well of us. Is there any man living who would feel no shame if all his life were made public? To compare English and African Christians fairly, it would be necessary to compare African Christians as they evidently are with English ones as they really are, all their private life made public; which, of course, it is impossible to do. I, for one, do not complain of Canon Taylor's denunciation of native converts' lives (though there are noble exceptions); only to be just, he should as sternly denounce the failings of Christians at home. Taking into consideration our enormous advantages in the way of education and surroundings, and our thirteen or fourteen centuries of hereditary morality, I do not think we shine when compared with African Christians; nor, on the contrary, do I think that they put us to shame.

I remember another case of a native convert; not an exceptional case, but like the preceding one, a very usual every-day one. This man was a native of Unyamwezi, a slave who had escaped many years before from a cruel master, and who had been brought to the knowledge of the truth under the successful labours of the missionary previously referred to. He used to spend his spare time in teaching the native children around to read the Bible, and used freely to give of his substance to feed those who came from a distance, as some did, to learn more of the good tidings, about which they had heard. He had a really affectionate wife, who was also a believer, and who helped him in his good works. Yet one day he quarrelled with her, left her, and went off with another wife. He was prayed for much by those whom he had left, and after a month or two he returned. He was told that he could not be taken back again as catechist until he had shown, as well as stated, that his repentance was real. After some months he was restored to his post. During this interval he had lived as a Christian should do, though very badly off, as he could get no work to do and was dependent on his wife for support. Previously to his reception he publicly confessed his fault in the little church. Since that date, now long ago, he has not again fallen away.

Another difficulty which besets the African convert, and which is second only in importance to his early training in vice, is his belief in witchcraft. But witchcraft is not so much an obstacle to the reception of Christianity as it is to the living of a consistent Christian life. Where it is believed in no man's life is safe; there is no sense of security from the ill-will of others, no true love towards them; each man feels, not only that he may be bewitched at any time, which is terrible enough, but also that he may be accused of bewitching others, and made to suffer the penalty, which is much more terrible; each man believes that it is in the power of his neighbour to tyrannize over him if he owe him any grudge. Living under such conditions as these is like living under a despotic monarchy, but with innumerable despots instead of one. Where witchcraft is, there is bitter hatred, envy, jealousy, revenge, and therefore no possibility of brotherly love, or of the charity which thinketh no evil; no possibility of the unity, the oneness which Christ came to bring, and which is the very evidence of Christianity to the outside world. And yet whilst admitting to the full the unspeakable evils of witchcraft, it nevertheless seems to me to be a mistake to attempt to combat directly any of the superstitious beliefs of the natives, for they are the result of mental as much as of moral darkness, and mental and moral light will disperse them. You cannot teach a child not to fear the dark if he has once been taught to be afraid of it. In the dark he is in dread of unknown dangers, and nothing but long experience of both day and night will convince him that the night has no added horrors over the day. As he gradually comes to know all the forces that are at work during the day, he will realize that they, and no others, are at work during the night also. So an African, after he embraces Christianity, will only gradually learn that God rules over the powers of heaven, earth, and hell in Africa as well as in other lands, that His are the cattle on a thousand hills, that His is the earth and the fulness thereof; and that so long as all things work together for good to them that love Him, no powers of witchcraft, no unlucky sequences of events can interfere with the welfare of one who has such protection as this. No actual test, no logical argument convinces him that an individual superstition is wrong; but as he gradually grasps the fact that the over-ruling control of God extends to all time and space, to the infinitely small, as well as to the infinitely great, he begins to realize that the belief in chance and luck and witchcraft are incompatible with his present knowledge; and the superstitions which once ruled his ideas, harassed his daily life and rendered anxious his nights, are gradually and imperceptibly eliminated by the expansion of his knowledge. There has been no violent tearing up of growths whose roots have hitherto ramified in every department of his life, no sudden extinguishing of beliefs which formerly smouldered in his heart to blaze up ever and anon in acts of hideous cruelty, but a gradual suppression by replacement. Trust in God and in His watchful and unvarying lovingkindness has destroyed his trust in witchcraft and chance. One fire has burnt out another's burning.

We have spoken before of the indifference of the people, but indifference is not a barrier to work. It retards, but does not otherwise interfere with success, unless, of course, it makes the missionary become disheartened, and so causes him to give up the work. Indifference only means that in any village you must go to the people instead of expecting them to come to you, and that when you have gone once without result, you must repeat the visit. It is usually best when going to them to commence by telling them the story of redemption; but it is useless to stop at that, as they already have an idea, and a wrong one, of what redemption means. Their idea of redemption is that a man buys a slave, and buys him simply for what he can get out of him; so that it is necessary at the same time to tell them what the life of the redeemed soul must be like, and what it will be like if faith be real.

Stupidity, or rather slowness, naturally prevalent amongst them, the accumulated product of centuries of unexercised faculties, is quite compensated for by its association with humility. Many of the natives are most genuinely humble, which is a great help. Whenever the Commandments of God are explained to them, they freely admit that they are unable to please Him. More than once have I known men say: 'We have been brought up as slaves and heathen, and we cannot keep steady.' Once, too, when we were arranging at a freed-slave station to apprentice boys to different trades, and were discussing with the leading natives the question as to what time should be allowed each boy to learn his trade, they at once said: 'You must give the boys a good deal longer to learn than you would give a white boy. The African heads are thick, and we don't take in things quickly.'

The method of work most favoured in Eastern Equatorial Africa is to establish a station at some convenient village, and itinerate from that as a centre. For a medical man it is necessary to live at one village. Little, if any good, can be done by itinerating medical work. The first essential, on settling at any place, is to build a good substantial house for protection from sun and rain. Such houses are easily built. The ground having been measured and levelled, uprights about six inches in diameter, and having forked tops, are put in at intervals of about a foot, except in the future doorways, to form the four walls. The two end walls are built of uprights gradually increasing in height towards the centre, and so are the partition walls between each room. Long, light, straight branches are now tied on to these uprights at right angles to them, both inside and outside, until the walls are converted into wickerwork. The inner bark of trees, cut into strips, is used as rope for tying this wickerwork. A strong pole, or else two spliced, are now placed to form the ridge of the roof, and from these long poles reach down to uprights placed some feet beyond the walls and enclosing a veranda between them. Upon these poles thin boughs or light bamboos are tied, and the framework of the roof is then thickly thatched. This being finished, and the structure beneath safe from rain, the space between the inner and outer wickerwork of the walls, except at the window places, is then filled in with stones, and the interstices filled in with clay, which is also used to plaster the inside and outside of the walls, and so give them a comparatively smooth surface. The exposed timber and wickerwork, where the windows are to be, are now cut away, and window-frames inserted. The floor is then beaten for some days to render it hard and smooth, and finally tarred to protect it from the ravages of the white ants, dry sand being poured over the tar to form a tougher coating than the tar alone would do, and to hasten the drying process. The walls are then white-washed inside and outside, a ceiling of calico stretched across beneath the thatch, mosquito netting stretched across the windows, a light canvas and woodwork door at the entrance, and curtains in the inside doorways, and the house is ready for inhabiting. Before building the house, it is best to char all the timbers that are to be used. This is really the only way to protect them from the ravages of the white ants, and of the far more troublesome and ubiquitous

House Building

boring beetles which, flying about everywhere, silently and quietly destroy every exposed piece of dry woodwork. A coating of tar or paint will restrain their ravages somewhat, but not nearly so

TEMPORARY AND PERMANENT HOUSES FOR EUROPEANS

effectually, and of course not nearly so economically, as a charred surface.

A small temporary house can be built in one or two days on the same plan as the preceding one, but with the roof timbers prolonged down to the ground, and so taking their support from it, and not from the walls or veranda uprights. The walls can thus be made very light, and with practically no foundation, as they are steadied by the roof, instead of having to support it. An outside covering only of wickerwork is tied on to the walls, which are then thatched like the roof. Of course this necessitates having the door and window in the end-walls, and taking care that long eaves shelter both ends from sun and rain.

When a native becomes an inquirer, the usual plan is for him to join a Bible-class for beginners, which would meet perhaps twice a week for the purpose of reading the Bible together and of prayer. The class for men and boys would be conducted by the missionary, and for women and girls by his wife. Both men and boys take their turn in reading and in leading in prayer—very different from the practice in England, where a boy's shyness and self-consciousness would usually keep him from praying in front of others. But natives, as we have seen, are quite accustomed to living their whole lives in front of each other, and have never yet heard of people being ridiculed for religious beliefs or observances, whether those observances be heathen, Mohammedan, or Christian. Disadvantageous as the shy-

The Convicter of Sin

ness and self-consciousness of an English boy may be in some ways, these very features place him on an elevation far above what the average native ever attains to. Modesty is a grace of tender growth, and shyness and reticence are her handmaidens. One obvious advantage which their unfettered way of praying gave them was that they learnt to pray for what they wanted in simple straightforward language, instead of praying for what they thought they ought to want in phraseology to be approved by the hearers, as is too often the case amongst more civilized people. More than once in their unsophisticated way they used to pray that I might get to know the language better in order to teach them more—perhaps at a time when I was rather flattering myself that I had a good grasp of it.

One thing that often puzzled me before I went out was the question occasionally put to me: 'How are you going to convince the natives of sin?' But convincing people of sin, whether white or coloured, is not our duty at all. It is solely the work of God's Holy Spirit who 'shall convince the world of sin.' Consequently I never took any steps in the matter. Certainly even the most degraded natives have some idea of sin. Although they will occasionally tell you that it is not wrong for them to steal and tell lies, yet they will at once admit, if you ask them, that it is very wrong for other people to steal from them or tell them lies. With regard to other sins not so obviously wrong, I used to read them God's commandments on the subject, but never attempted to argue the advisability of such commands. Nor was proof usually called for. The mere fact that an action was forbidden in a book which professed to come from God was frequently to them an end of all discussion. They may not have intended to obey; but they rarely, if ever, disputed the validity of the order. The lowest orders of intellect seem to realize the sinfulness of their lives quite as clearly as the more quick-witted. I remember one man—the most stupid we had on the station—who attended the usual morning and evening prayers, but who apparently gained no benefit from the teaching then given. Yet one day of his own accord he presented himself at the inquirers' class asking for instruction previous to baptism, and surprised both us and his fellow-natives, not only by his evident earnestness, but also by the simplicity and clearness with which he had grasped what his own condition before God really was, and what was necessary for salvation. He was willingly admitted to the class.

Two or three days later there broke out one of those troublesome epidemics due to the fouling of the water-supply, and he was the first victim.

About the same time as the preceding occurrence, another man, much more intelligent, was also brought to the knowledge of the truth, and earnestly applied himself to the task of learning to read that he might, when he returned to his own tribe, who lived some four hundred miles away, be able to tell them the good news that he had heard. Before he had thoroughly learnt to read, his teacher had to remove from that station to the coast; and as an opportunity came of his returning to his tribe in a passing caravan, he went earlier than he otherwise would have done. But although he could not read properly even when he left, he yet knew a good deal of his Bible. What results he is now getting from his work amongst his fellow-tribesmen in the far interior time alone will reveal. This man was one of the most truthful men I have ever met, either in England or abroad; and his guilelessness was all the more noticeable amidst the proverbial and prevalent untruthfulness and craft of the native African. He was indeed one whose words and actions were exact reflections of the thoughts within.

The belief in witchcraft once brought us into contact with a native chief in a very unexpected way. He had been ailing for some time with rheumatism, and as he slept in a draughty, leaky hut, it was not surprising that medicines had little effect in allaying his malady. Dissatisfied with his condition, however, he sent over the hills for a native medicine man, who on his arrival told him, as was customary, that the cause of his malady was that he was being bewitched. He then commenced casting the customary lots from door to door and from native to native, until he hit upon a poor old slave man and woman, who were thereupon hacked to death with native axes. Some of the natives who were well disposed came up to the mission and told us what had occurred, adding that, according to the medicine man's orders, one or two people would be put to death every day until the chief recovered. So we went up to see the old man, who received us politely, as usual. We told him of what we had heard, and how sorry we were to know of the course which he had taken. We told him that man might try to alleviate his disease, but that really it was God alone who could cure him. To this he readily agreed, as it is the belief which most natives have. Then we reminded him that all his people belonged to the Creator, who made all men and all things. To this he also assented. 'Then is it not unwise to go on killing God's people, while you are desiring Him to save your life?' After some deliberation, he promised to kill no more people; so one point was gained, and the lives saved of two poor innocent young girls who were marked out as the victims for the next day. But it was only one point gained, for we wanted the poor deluded old man to acknowledge his fault and obtain forgiveness too, and so we spoke to him of what God said of those who killed their fellow-creatures. He would not admit that he had done anything wrong, so we had to be content with the one important point we had gained and return home. Next day we saw him again and had another talk with him, and he so far relented as to admit that he had done wrong. Some days later, when we were again visiting him, he said that he was very sorry for what he had done, and wished to know if God would forgive him. We told him that confession with sorrow was always followed by forgiveness; but that as his sin had been committed openly, and as he had thus set a bad example to all, his confession ought to be equally open. Then he said he would confess in front of all. But he was too ill to go out and see his people, so he agreed to call together his under-chiefs, and those who had seen the crime committed, and to confess before them. This was in the evening, so he said that he would do it in the morning. It was such a very trying act for a chief, who was supposed by his subjects never to do wrong, openly to confess a sin before them; it was so much like admitting that he was not fit to be a chief, that I much doubted if he really meant to call his men together. However, early next morning, about six o'clock, two of his men came down to say that the under-chiefs and others were already collected at his hut, at which we were much surprised, as some of them lived two miles away, and the old chief must have been very much in earnest to get the men together so soon. We at once went up to his hut, and then he sat up in his bed, and told his assembled subjects that he had done wrong in killing two innocent people, and that he had called us all together that we might all ask God to forgive him for the wrong he had done. I suppose it was the first prayer that most of these heathen had ever offered up, as we all knelt down and asked God's forgiveness for the old chief and for all present, as we were all sinners in His sight.

We saw the old chief a few times after that; but each time he was weaker. On the last occasion on which I was with him, I read the one hundred and third psalm to him; he stopped me at the words 'like as a father pitieth his children,' and said: 'Is that the way God looks upon us? I never knew that before.' Soon after this he died, and his men came down to the mission, and told us the news the same night. They told us in strict confidence; as, when a chief dies, the matter is kept quiet until his successor is appointed—a matter sometimes of one or two months—as apparently many formalities have to be gone through.

Amongst boys, it is not indifference, but instability of character which is the great trouble. They are wanting in backbone, which is hardly surprising in a country where there are few or no moral laws. Yet they have redeeming features, for though they are lazy, idle and dishonest, yet they are merry, good-natured, and not cowardly; indeed, I have sometimes been surprised at the pluck of many of the little boys. I have known a couple of little fellows of ten and eleven with their small spears go off to the rescue of one of their flock that was being attacked by a leopard, and succeed in driving it away. On another occasion, when some Germans were attacking a village at which one of their men had been murdered; and when two of us had to go down a hill between the opposing forces, to endeavour to bring them to terms peaceably, one or two little boys of six or seven followed us down all the way, not fearing to go where they saw us go, even though the bullets came faster and faster, whistling across the path which led us down to the combatants.

Some of the boys, who come completely under the control of the missionary, turn out very fine fellows. A slave-boy who had run away from a cruel master, was received at a mission station, and there brought up and taught by Mr. Downes Shaw. He became a consistent believer, and was baptized. His master, who discovered his whereabouts, after a good deal of negotiating, consented to his freedom being purchased, which was effected by the boy himself out of his own savings. He became a most earnest worker amongst his fellow-countrymen, and now works as catechist amongst them on very small wages, having, for that purpose, given up work in which he was very happy, and at which he gained twice or thrice as much as his present allowance. I know of others who are doing similar work under like conditions.

CHAPTER XII

THE MISSIONARY (*continued*)

WORK amongst the Mohammedans of the coast is exceedingly difficult; yet I believe that many amongst them are now truly earnest followers of Christ; though it is impossible to estimate their numbers. The detractors of missions sometimes assert that there are none; but this is obviously erroneous, as there are men, now in orders as clergymen of the Church of England, who once were Mohammedans. Yet if even Elijah could say: 'And I, only, am left,' when there were seven thousand people who had not bowed the knee to Baal, it is not surprising if many think the same now. To a Mohammedan, the open profession of his belief in Christ, whilst he is living in his own country, means the loss of all whom he loves, and almost certain starvation, unless the mission under whose teaching he was converted gives him work enough to support him. But the rule to give lucrative employment to a man directly he becomes a professing Christian, has obvious disadvantages.

I knew one Mohammedan young man, who, after attending our services for some time, said that he wanted to have his sins forgiven, and to follow Isa (Jesus). He joined the inquirers' class, and was very humble and simple in his prayers, and very careful in his life. After a period of probation, he was baptized, and became a consistent believer. During the war between the Germans and Arabs, when an Arab chief ordered all white men and their servants to be killed, he left us, and went back to his Mohammedan friends. I saw him once afterwards, and he said that he was afraid to come to us again, but that he would not give up the worship of Isa, and that he was not worshipping in Mohammedan mosques. And so he remains, like other nominal Mohammedan friends of mine, and like those many Israelites in the time of Ahab and Jezebel, a secret and unknown believer. It is not a high position to occupy; but let those who have successfully resisted such fearful temptations as beset a Mohammedan who gives up the religion of his forefathers, cast the first stone at him.

It is sometimes asserted, and usually, though not always, by those who have never lived amongst the

Africans, that Mohammedanism is more suited to the African nature than Christianity; and that there is no reason why their acceptance of it should not take them halfway towards, and finally lead them actually into Christianity. In the consideration of this subject, it will, I think, help us if we divide the Africans into the following six classes: 1. The civilized truly Christian. 2. The civilized nominally Christian. 3. The semi-civilized heathen. 4. The uncivilized heathen. 5. The semi-civilized true Mohammedan. 6. The semi-civilized nominal Mohammedan.

Theoretically there should be other classes, such as 'the uncivilized true Mohammedan,' etc., but practically such classes do not exist, at any rate in East Central Africa. In this list I have drawn a distinction between real and nominal—a distinction obviously often difficult to draw in practice in individual cases. Yet the distinction is a real and important one, and indeed often an evident one. Let me define my meaning. By a true Christian, I understand to be meant one who accepts Christ as his Saviour and Master, and who does desire to follow his commands; who tries and perhaps fails, and fails again, until in some cases his life comes almost to be considered a life of failures. It may be, but it is also a life of attempts. By a nominal Christian I understand to be meant one who, whatever may be his profession, has evidently no desire to follow the commands of Christ; and who never has had any such desires, beyond the most transitory ones.

The African Christian, so far as I know him, is very far above the African Mohammedan in truthfulness, honesty, and love towards his neighbour, further above him in these characteristics than the Mohammedan is above the heathen. But he is not above, indeed often below, the Mohammedan in courtesy, deference to his superiors, and sometimes in obedience to his master; the very traits by which the critic is apt to judge him. But whilst this is correct of the true Christian African, the nominal one is distinctly below the Mohammedan in all of the characteristics we have enumerated, and is often more troublesome and more offensive than even the heathen. The reason of this is not far to seek. Christianity and civilization are always presented at one and the same time to the African mind. The native who imbibes Christianity, unlike the native who imbibes Mohammedanism, never imbibes it alone; but in obtaining Christianity from his teacher, he, at the same time, obtains the rudiments of civilization. The nominal Christian, who drinks from the same fountain as the true one, rejects Christianity; but yet gets, with his imperfect knowledge of it, a fair grounding in the rudiments of civilization, and that a true civilization, not the semi-civilization of the Arabs. This civilization, divorced from Christianity, does not, as a rule, better him, and often renders him, if not worse, at least more dangerous to the white man. The dishonest, ignorant, timid heathen becomes the equally dishonest, but more clever, more crafty, more insolent nominal Christian. It is a change like that from the half-witted, ignorant rustic, who would be dishonest if he dared, to the well-trained card-sharper, who is dishonest because he does dare. An outside observer would praise the honesty of the rustic, and condemn the sharper; yet one is not worse than the other, though he is more dangerous to society, more objectionable to the wealthy, and therefore universally condemned. In reading the strictures sometimes passed by travellers and settlers upon both nominal and real Christian natives, when they assert that the heathen are better men than the converts, one must bear in mind that often all they mean by a good native is one who is obedient and moderately honest, and who only gets drunk when his master does not want him. As to any other goodness, such as honour, purity, and unselfishness, he is not supposed to be capable of it, even if it were desirable that he should possess it.

The semi-civilized heathen is practically the same as the preceding type of native; no better and no worse. The nominal Christian, though often a hypocrite, may style himself a Christian without any conscious hypocrisy; or he may, even in consideration of his civilized condition, be styled so by his friends and neighbours who consider civilization and Christianity identical, without any desire for the name on his own part. On the other hand, the heathen, though he does not hypocritically set up for being a Christian, may yet, just as insincerely, endeavour to assure you that he is the incarnation of truth and honour and unselfishness, when he is quite aware that he sets no value at all upon these 'white man's peculiarities,' as he considers them.

The uncivilized heathen native hardly needs description here. He is described throughout this book. He can hardly fairly be described as a class comparable with the other five classes; he is rather to be considered the raw material from which the other classes are recruited. This being the case, he is necessarily never so good as the best of the individuals we are considering, and never so bad as the worst. It is, I think, from amongst the best of the heathen that the true Christians are recruited. A priori, I think I should have expected to see more of the worst attracted to a system whose ranks are recruited largely by those brought in from the highways and hedges; but perhaps the men from hedges and ditches mean honest workmen. Certainly amongst the Africans it is those who already have, if not good in them, at least good desires, that yield themselves most readily as followers of Christ. It is the kind-hearted and the gentle, the (comparatively) hard-working and the honest who come forward as inquirers, not the vicious and the outcast, the villain or the brute.

Now let us turn to the Mohammedan; and, in the first place, take the instance of the semi-civilized true Mohammedan. He would almost certainly belong to the coast, as the externals of Mohammedanism, and the association with other Mohammedans necessary to kindle and to keep up the fire of enthusiasm, would hardly be obtainable anywhere in the interior. The first feature that strikes one about a true Mohammedan is his evident sincerity, a by no means unimportant feature. 'I obtained mercy,' said St. Paul, 'because I did it ignorantly in unbelief;'

and one of the latest recorded utterances of the Son of God was that He hated those who were neither hot nor cold. Not only is the Mohammedan sincere, but he is more self-respectful, more courteous, more obedient, more truthful, and more trustful of others than the heathen is. When dealing with heathen you realize the great disadvantage of working with people who do not trust you, until after they have known you individually, and that for a long time. In dealing with Mohammedans, on the contrary, you are dealing with those who do trust you. It says a great deal for a man when he trusts other people. It means that he must have a belief in such things as truth and honesty. And a man who has such a belief as this is capable of higher things than a man who has not. But whilst Mohammedanism teaches a man his duty towards others, it does not teach him that he has any duty at all except towards a small portion of his fellow-creatures. It makes him despise, and often hate, the rest of mankind. It does not tend much to diminish his evil passions, though it does make them run in more regular channels; and impure though a Mohammedan may be, he is, I believe, considerably above a heathen, even in this respect. The most awkward feature that an Englishman finds in a Mohammedan's character is his fanaticism. Valuable though a Mohammedan often is in the capacity of a personal servant, he cannot be trusted when there is war between Christians and Mohammedans, or even when his master has a disagreement with some neighbouring Mohammedan of position or influence.

The preceding description of a Mohammedan native, accurate though I believe it is, has yet one weak point in it. It is taken from observation of half-Arabs, the offspring of Arab fathers and native mothers. I have been obliged to substitute the half-Arab for the native, for I do not know any single instance in Eastern Equatorial Africa of a pure native who has become a true and earnest Mohammedan. But whilst there are no (or very few) true and earnest Mohammedan natives, there are many nominal ones, who do not, as a class, correspond with those I have described as nominal Christians. The nominal Mohammedan cares practically nothing for religious rites, and never performs them when alone, nor when in company, unless in the presence of an Arab. Such a man is naturally free from fanaticism, yet he does learn something of the rules of conduct that guide Mohammedans, and he is comparatively unspoilt by civilization; for the Arab, unlike the missionary, does not take much civilization with him, and his converts consequently get practically none. Thus, though the nominal Mohammedan is inferior to the true Mohammedan in many points of conduct, yet he is decidedly above the heathen; and his freedom from fanaticism makes him much more valuable to his Christian employer than the true Mohammedan would be in times of disagreement between Christians and Mohammedans.

Supposing all this description is correct, say some, yet is not Mohammedanism more suited to the native African than Christianity? Speaking only from experience in Eastern Equatorial Africa, the practical absence of true Mohammedan natives would be a sufficient answer to this question; but nominal Mohammedanism being, as we have seen, so much more desirable a condition than heathenism, we are unwilling to urge the former fact as at all a conclusive reply. No doubt it is easier for the African to govern himself by the few rules set forth by Mohammedanism, and to control the few passions which that system insists shall be controlled, than to govern himself by the all-embracing stringent laws of Christianity. But the same holds good for us; we should find it much easier to obey the laws of Mohammed than the laws of Christ, though of

The Best System

course our own ease would be purchased at the cost of that of our fellow-creatures. The whole question thus narrows itself to this: Is the African capable of Christianity? Or in other words: May it not be better to teach him an imperfectly pure system which he can follow rather than a perfectly pure one which he cannot? Now, it is quite easy to teach an African what his duty is, whether as a Mohammedan or as a Christian; though, obviously, to enable him to act upon this knowledge is a totally different thing. The matter thus turns upon whether either or both systems give not only commands, but strength to fulfil them. Now Mohammedanism, though it does not give its devotees the strength to fulfil its commands, yet only gives such commands as are compatible with even an African's moral strength; but Christianity, which gives commands far beyond the power of the natural man to fulfil, does give with them the strength necessary for their fulfilment. God gives grace to His followers in proportion to their needs, and has promised His Holy Spirit to those of His children who ask Him. Without God's Holy Spirit the African would certainly be unequal to the task, but so would the cultivated Englishman, though with His aid both are sufficient.

Here again, however, we are met by a fresh perplexity. If these things are so, if it is good for a heathen to become even a nominal Mohammedan, and if that change is attainable and fairly sure, why should we not encourage natives to accept Mohammedanism as a probable stage in the journey towards Christianity. There is undoubtedly something to be said in favour of this view. Those who have talked both with non-fanatical Mohammedans and with heathen, know how much more receptive, how much more appreciative of the true and the noble, how much more approachable, a Mohammedan is than a heathen. But although to convince a Mohammedan seems easier than to convince a heathen, yet to get him to confess his belief is far harder. The penalties are so fearful that a Mohammedan, in a Mohammedan country or district, hardly dares to take even the first step of allowing himself to say, even in secret, that Christianity is true. Such a confession would mean one man against the world, and though Mohammedans capable of such heroism can be found, I am afraid that they are not only few and far between, but that they are quickly put out of the way. If some Mohammedan ruler were to accept Christianity, and a few of the leading mollahs with him, the probability is that many Mohammedans would accept Christianity at once. When a heathen king becomes a Christian, all his subjects follow suit, as a matter of course, and nominal Christianity, worth very little, becomes the order of the day. But if a Mohammedan potentate and court were to accept Christianity, I believe that the result would be a large number of real and not merely of nominal Christians. But such an event as this, I am afraid, is in the highest degree unlikely.

Willingly then as we admit the really good and desirable features of Mohammedanism when compared with heathenism, naturally as we might at first imagine that with its purer creed and nobler life it might be a handmaid to Christianity, we yet cannot shut our eyes to the fact that practically it is not so, and that the persecuting tenets inseparably bound up with the system of Mohammedanism far more than neutralize any assistance which it might otherwise lend to the cause of Christianity.

The knowledge of medicine is of great use in working amongst the Arabs and natives of the coast, and it gives a missionary the entrée of houses that he would otherwise never have an opportunity of entering, and brings him into friendly relations with people whom he would otherwise never know. But for this coast work in such semi-civilized regions, it needs a competent medical man, and not one who simply has a smattering of medical knowledge. To obtain the confidence of the Arabs and natives, is of great advantage in the work, even if one does not obtain their gratitude. Of their confidence, a discreet medical man can make fairly sure; but gratitude is an uncertain factor in any calculation; civilized people are not always grateful for even great attention, and when the pain is over, some few forget to pay the doctor, which, no doubt, led the canny Scotch practitioner to say:

> 'Get your fee
> While the tear's in the e'e.'

At the time even when feeling against white people was running so high in East Africa, during the blockade of the coast by the combined British and German squadrons, the Arabs were always willing to come for medical aid to the mission stations; even the very Arab chief, who was threatening a mission station, came to that very station to consult the doctor there about an operation for a complaint from which he was suffering. But though at the coast only a thoroughly competent knowledge of medicine is of much use, in the far interior matters are different. There a man who has even a smattering only of medical knowledge, provided that smattering is practical and includes the rudiments of nursing, can do a great deal of good. If he can treat and nurse cases of typhoid fever, dysentery, malarial fever, and bronchitis, and dress simple wounds and ulcers, he will be able to do most that is required of him, especially if he has the good sense not to meddle with what he does not understand.

There is one use of medical knowledge in the mission-field that I think needs a word of caution. Medical knowledge used merely to impress the natives with the idea of the superior intellect and powers of the missionary will probably only result in the native putting him on a par with the medicine-man or wizard. And so the missionary will encourage the very belief which it is his aim to combat. One occasionally hears it stated in meetings at home, and sometimes even in sober print, that the medical missionary is the only one who fulfils the Christian ideal, the only one who in his methods of work resembles his Master. This idea seems to have arisen from a total misapprehension of the function of medical knowledge in missionary efforts. The Lord did work *miracles* of healing, and pointed men to His miracles as evidence that He had supernatural power and that He was Divine. We have no supernatural power, and do not want to point men to ourselves. Medical missionaries are very fortunate in possessing knowledge gained by observation—knowledge which often enables them to relieve physical pain, and so gives them more opportunities than others of helping people; but there the difference between them and others ends. If a man tries to impress people with the idea that he has occult powers, whether he be a quack in England or a medical missionary in foreign lands, he is simply acting a conscious lie. I always found it best wherever I went to endeavour at once to disabuse the native mind of the idea that I possessed any powers over nature beyond those granted to ordinary intelligent observation. 'Some of you good people can snare birds with great success. And why? Are you wizards? No; but you have spent many years in observing the habits of birds and in experimenting with the different structures with which traps can be made. The result is the very ingenious and complicated traps which are made by you Africans, and the successful way in which you discover the time and place to set them. And so we white doctors have spent many years in observing diseases, and in experimenting with the herbs and appliances which will allay those diseases.' There is far more gained, from a missionary's point of view, in nursing and caring for one native than in administering the magic draught and never-failing pill to several hundred. True, you are a marvellous man, and can cure the diseases of people who come to you. But the native doctor is a much more marvellous man. By simple incantations he can not only cure people, but make them ill, and that at a distance. But when it comes to nursing and caring for the sick, then the white doctor can have the monopoly if he so desires. The native knows a hundred other doctors who outshine the white one by their marvellous feats, but he knows not one other who will lend him a blanket and cook him some arrowroot when he is cold and hungry and ill.

The majority of natives in Africa come to their end through cold and hunger, a fact little realized by those who hear that the temperature rarely goes below sixty degrees Fahrenheit, and that food is usually abundant. But whilst such a temperature as that mentioned is bearable to a man in health, it means death in a very short time to an underclothed man with severe fever or dysentery, or, indeed, any acute disease. And the coarse food which can be eaten with impunity in health is unpalatable and often dangerous in sickness. Blankets, flannel shirts, and woollen belts are thus more necessary to a medical missionary than almost any other article. A native, it is true, does not need the same comforts in sickness that a European does; but he does need that there shall be as great a difference between his comforts in health and disease as there is between those of a European in similar circumstances.

Medical skill being an unknown and consequently unvalued commodity in Central Africa, the medical man who goes there must not expect to be at once surrounded by sick folk all thirsting for his assistance. He must be content to abide by the same laws that rule in other departments of political economy; and in introducing to their notice such a new article as medical skill, he must be prepared, not only to provide the commodity, but also to create the demand for it. This he can only effect by gentleness and by patient dealing with the few who come to him at first, some with incurable ailments, some with trifling, and many with altogether imaginary, ones.

Situated as Mpwapwa is at the junction of many of the great East Central African slave-routes, a

Hospital Huts

medical man living there naturally obtained many patients from the passing caravans. Those so obtained were, of course, absolutely destitute, and needed to be provided, not only with medicine, but also with clothing, food, and lodging. For lodging them we found that it was cheapest to house them

HUTS FOR SICK NATIVES

by twos, building for this purpose a sort of large beehive, six feet high, and seven feet in diameter at the base. This was built of a light framework of boughs, and thatched outside right down to the ground. Two six-foot logs parallel to each other were then laid along the floor inside, leaving a space between them for a wood-fire for warmth at night, and having the spaces between each of them and the hut walls filled with dried grass to form a soft bed. A few thorns twisted into the thatch outside at the base of the wall all round prevented hyenas from scratching through any unprotected part at night. These little huts only cost about seven shillings each, and they were especially useful for isolating infectious cases, as the hut could be burnt down without much loss of money as soon as the patient was well.

All patients so destitute as those of whom we have been speaking had necessarily to be treated gratis; but if possible, we usually found it advisable to make others pay something for the benefits they received, even if it were only a banana, worth the twentieth part of a penny. I am convinced that it is a mistake to pauperize people, whether in Central Africa or in England, by giving them for half-price what they can afford to pay for in full, or by giving them for nothing what they can afford to pay for in part, though, of course, there will always remain a certain number who cannot afford to pay anything, even for the necessaries of life. An inquiring, discriminating charity causes more work and trouble to the giver than either indiscriminate almsgiving or the complete refusal to give unpaid assistance; but it is the only really kind unselfish way, the only way that is likely to result in good to the recipient without any attendant harm.

We have not yet considered the relation of the missionary to the work of the civilization of the people. There have been high civilizations in the past coupled with the most degrading and immoral customs; so that one can hardly look to civilization as the necessary antecedent to a moral change in the people. Consul O'Neill, when considering this subject, says: 'Most valuable though a religious training is, it does not seem to reach alone the weaknesses of the native character; and its effects—judged by experience—appear to be sadly evanescent and volatile. . . . The one thing most wanting in the native temperament is stability; and this want is best met, not by theoretical teaching, but by habits of practical and regular industry.' I think all workers in the African field will agree with Consul O'Neill that the one thing most wanting is 'stability'; and where the young are committed to the missionary's charge, as in the case of freed slave children, most would agree that they should be trained up in regular habits of industry, the few who show special aptitude being perhaps given a literary training; but the majority being brought up to do mechanical work, and as far as possible, apprenticed to different trades. This is done by the Universities' Mission in Zanzibar and the adjacent mainland, and by the Church Missionary Society at Frere Town. So far, then, as the young are concerned, we shall all be of one mind with Consul O'Neill in his desire that 'no mission be established in Africa which is not mainly of an industrial nature'; but when the question of work amongst adults is considered, we shall not by any means find such an unanimity of opinion. For my own part, I look upon the attempt to civilize those past early adult age as a hopeless task when undertaken by itself. The African who has grown up to full maturity in heathen customs does not want to be civilized, does not want to work, and you cannot oblige him to as you can the younger people. The only prospect, so far as I can see, of ever getting him to work hard, and lead a sober, orderly life, is by first getting him converted. If an African has the love of God in his heart, he will get desires towards higher things than he naturally seeks after, and his civilization will go hand in hand with his growth in spiritual life. Whether a civilized African would receive the Gospel more readily than an uncivilized one, I do not in the least know. But my small experience, as far as it goes, certainly gives me the right to expect that the Christian African will embrace civilization a great deal more easily and naturally than the heathen one. To attempt to civilize the African before attempting to convert him is, I think, to put the cart before the horse; yet there are others who differ from me on this question, and, of course, their opinions are entitled to as much respect as my own.

There is one interesting and practical question with which we may well occupy ourselves for a short time, namely: What are the qualities that best fit a man for work in the mission field? Before I went out, I think I should have put purity and truthfulness first and other qualities after; but now since I have seen the work for myself, I think I should put affection for the people first. I have known men really fond of the natives, who were nevertheless most unrefined in their behaviour, and rather shifty to deal with, and yet who were distinctly successful in their work. The opposite condition of a refined, straightforward man who did not care for the natives is not to be found; for such a man if he went out would be quickly disgusted with the work, and give it up. Again, bad temper is not such an obstacle to success as I, for one, should have imagined. I knew one man who had a very quick temper, and who was constantly storming at his servants; and telling natives, who certainly deserved his censure, precisely what he thought of them. But he was a man of great culture and refinement, and loved the natives with a true affection—a love which they returned; and his ministry was eminently successful. Unfortunately the bad qualities we have been considering, the first two more especially, are not often combined with this necessary kindheartedness, and so the unrefined man is frequently the unsuccessful one. The refined cultured man is undoubtedly the man best suited for work amongst such a degraded people as the Africans; he will stoop to their level, and they will learn to love him very quickly, and it is not hard to return love so readily given. The unrefined man will not stoop to their level so easily and naturally, paradoxical as this may seem. Yet it agrees with what an Indian missionary told me. 'The greatest help one can have in India is a converted Brahmin. He will go about as an equal amongst the very sweepers, the lowest caste of all; and is, consequently, such a useful worker, and so completely in possession of the confidence of all. A convert from an intermediate caste is not nearly so useful as a rule. He is frequently so afraid of losing dignity if he associates too much with those of lower caste.' But though men of culture and refinement may be, as a rule, the most successful missionaries, not many of this class have gone out until of late; and so most of the burden and heat of the day in pioneer mission work has been borne by men drawn from other classes, and to them it is largely due that the mission work of the present day is so much easier than that of the past.

Of women's work amongst the East African natives, I have said very little. Except in the Universities' Mission, this phase of work is almost in its infancy. Yet work amongst the native women and young children is hopeless when undertaken by men; and certainly will have to be undertaken by women, and the greater part of it by those who have not young children of their own. An Englishwoman in a tropical climate, with children of her own to manage, and only able to obtain the assistance which a missionary's pay can ensure, will be able to manage little work, as a rule, beyond that entailed by her own household; though happily she can undertake some, as much of the work amongst married women can be best effected by one who is a wife and a mother herself. A woman has many advantages over a man in missionary work. No one is suspicious of her, and she has the entrée to every place she cares to go to; so that although she cannot travel as far as a man, or stay so long in the climate, or stand a rough life so well, she can make as many friends in a one-mile circle as he can in a ten-mile one, and attract people to her whom neither medical knowledge nor any other aid will enable him to attract. But she must be one who has attracted people to her at home, before she goes abroad. No greater mistake can be made than to send abroad to mission work a woman whom no one, or whom very few will miss at home. People sometimes say: 'Oh, what a pity So-and-So went abroad, she was doing so much good at home.' But it is just the women who *are* doing good at home that are needed abroad. If a women does not love those whom she has seen, and who are of her own colour, she is not likely to love or be loved by those whom she has not seen, and who are not of her colour. If I might be allowed to give a word of advice to those who have not found their vocation in work at home, and who contemplate engaging in mission work abroad, I should say for the sake of the natives, and for the sake of your fellow-missionaries, by all means do not go.

The question has not infrequently been raised as to the advisability of missionaries living in poverty. I do not understand why a different standard should be laid down for Christian workers in England and in foreign lands. I think each man should be left to decide for himself. Personally I cannot say that I have taken the slightest interest in seeing how little I could live upon. Once, by a combination of circumstances, I was reduced to living upon nothing but muddy water for a week. It certainly resulted in great economy as regards that week's expenditure; but in anything but economy as regards the expenditure of the next three months. In a tropical climate a European must eat well, or he will soon lose his health; and he will find it very difficult if not impossible to eat a sufficient amount of tasteless or unpalatable food. To live poorly is bad economy. One month's illness costs directly and indirectly far more than a year's supply of comforts. I always endeavoured to live as well as I could; but still, except when at the coast, I would gladly have exchanged the food I was usually able to get for the ordinary diet of an English workhouse. I do not know any luxuries that will take the place of moderately tender meat, potatoes, bread and butter; yet for months the missionary may be called upon to go without all these. I have often been amused at hearing workhouse children objecting to meat as being tough, and bread as not fresh enough, and wondered what they would say to no bread, and a steak of Central African cow.

No doubt there might, in some instances, be more economy than there is amongst missionaries. But many a man in a comfortable position at home, who goes out into the mission field, has to give up about seventy per cent. of his income by so doing, and though he might possibly live on still less than he does, the philanthropist who is enjoying all the comforts of home life in a temperate region, and who uses perhaps ten per cent. of his income for others, is not exactly the right man to suggest his giving up seventy-five instead of seventy per cent.

So far as I can see it is the missionary's wife and children that are usually the sufferers. Some societies discountenance marriage amongst their missionaries, and those that do so are perhaps justified in not looking too closely into the needs of unprofitable widows and children; but others approve or even encourage marriage, and I think amongst these there is room for a diminution in the allowances to the missionary in the field, and a great augmentation in the allowances to widows and children. I am always sorry when I see the question of economy in missions brought very prominently forward; not because there is not room for economy, but because I always fear that it will simply mean more hardships and sufferings for women and children.

The last question that need detain us is the very important one as to whether or no missions are a success considering the time and money spent upon them. Eastern Equatorial Africa has sometimes been selected as a field, showing that they are not a success. But in such an early period of mission work in the interior, it is impossible (except in the case of Uganda and some of the Universities' Mission stations) to obtain sufficient statistics to base a conclusion upon—a conclusion, I mean, which shall carry weight to one unfamiliar with the practical details and difficulties of Central African mission work. As far as regards my own work out there, I quite feel that the return I obtained was fully equal to the amount and value of the work I did. One instance is not, of course, worth much; but others, whose work I have seen, bear out my belief that the evident result in each case has been commensurate with the efforts put forth. Then, there is much result which does not at first appear

—a harvest which will be reaped by later comers, and this also tells against the value of statistics on the subject, and makes it still more a matter of opinion. But the fact that those who are in the field, and alone have an opportunity of judging, are satisfied that the work is not a failure, makes the opinion of those who believe in missionary work more in accord with evidence than the opinion of those who do not. As to the money value of the results obtained, as I do not in the least know how to estimate missionary work in terms of current coin, I have not attempted to discuss the matter.

Whatever opinion may be held as to the present success or failure of Central African missions, the man who believes in God's message to us as to the evangelization of the world will go on working whilst others discuss. The war is still raging, and it ill becomes the soldier to sit down in the trenches whilst he calculates whether the battle in the past has been sufficiently successful to warrant him in obeying his Commander's orders to continue the attack.

Mission work in East Equatorial Africa is carried on at present at a great disadvantage, and must continue to be until there are a sufficient number of well-educated, well-trained, whole-hearted native converts ready themselves to carry the Gospel to their heathen brethren. The Universities' Mission, especially, has laboured towards the attainment of this end, and so of late years has the Church Missionary Society. Yet, notwithstanding the fewness of the labourers, though the whole work is still in its infancy, the results are really great. When we think of the centuries that passed between the first introduction of Christianity into England and its final establishment here, and of the years that were spent in educating the few descendants of Abraham during the first century after the call of that Patriarch, whilst the world around still lay in heathen darkness, we begin to realize that the work of God never progresses hurriedly, but ever with measured tread. In any great undertaking it is those that come later that reap the bulk of the harvest sown by the earlier workers who themselves reaped but a few first fruits. But whatever the apparent results, to each, according to his work, will one day be his meed of praise. To each of us is held out the promise that we may one day hear, not 'Well done, good and *successful*,' but 'Well done, good and *faithful* servant, enter thou into the joy of thy Lord'—the joy, that is, of a Successful Worker.

APPENDIX

LIST OF SUPPLIES NECESSARY FOR ONE PERSON TRAVELLING IN CENTRAL AFRICA FOR ONE YEAR

One tent, 8 ft. or 9 ft. square, with fly, and extra ceiling inside, of dark green baize.

Unjointed poles. Four small blunt hooks along centre of roof (just under supporting-tapes) for supporting lamps, etc. Two pockets in each side wall of tent.

Ventilators in roof.

One ground-sheet to cover whole floor of tent.

Eyelets along edge.

One canvas camp bedstead, with unjointed poles.

One Willesden canvas bag, open at one end only for bedstead.

The green Willesden rot-proof canvas tents, supplied by Edgington, of Duke Street, London Bridge, are excellent.

Unjointed poles are stronger and easier to carry.

The extra ceiling is very necessary. The sun comes through two thicknesses of canvas, and the shelter of trees is not often obtainable.

Willesden canvas is very good for this purpose. Very light, white-ant proof, and sufficiently waterproof.

The eyelets enable it to be used as an extra tent-covering for the men in wet weather, when no villages are near.

An extra pole for stability is sometimes supplied to connect angles where legs of bedstead cross. As natives cannot arrange it, it becomes an encumbrance.

Sufficiently large to hold bedstead rolled up with two or three blankets.

One *very* easy folding-chair. The seat and back should not be in one piece, as the resulting curve is not restful to the back.

If the traveller has fever he will spend days in this chair.

Two camp-stools. Strong, low, with wide seat.

One small, strong, *low* portable table. Fastened by a strap, or by some method which does not cause the table to collapse when it is *lifted by the top*. Most portable tables unfortunately do so.

One strap, with hooks (portable wardrobe) to fasten round tent-pole. The traveller should see that it fits when purchasing it.

One ribbed hair mattress.
Two small pillows.
Four pillow-cases.
Two pair of sheets.

This kind is light, soft, portable, and not expensive.

It is more cleanly and more comfortable to use a sheet to lie upon; but they are not used as coverings.

Six blankets. Austrian blankets spoil least by being washed by a native.

Mosquito net, arranged on cane ribs, in shape like the hood of a perambulator, but 2 ft. 3 in. wide, and half instead of one-quarter circle. It should have a linen fringe all round to tuck in. This is the most portable form of mosquito net. It covers the head and arms. The feet must be covered by a light shawl or rug.

There are few mosquitoes, except near the coast; but there they abound.

One dressing-case, well-fitted. To include mirror.

One india-rubber camp-bath, whalebone ribs. Will stand about a year of camp wear under a tropical sun if the traveller always puts it away *dry*, and keeps it free from grease.

Two sponges.
One sponge-bag.

One bass broom-head. This will save many minutes in preparing the ground for the floor of the tent.

Two dusting-brushes. Very useful.

One gallon tin water-bottle, with screwed top. To be kept filled with boiled water, and given to be car-

Filters

One ebonite flask, or flask of other light material.	ried by a lightly-laden, quick porter, who will be in camp each day as soon as the traveller.
One portable filter—metal.	To be kept filled with boiled water, and carried by servant who carries traveller's gun. Not less than one quart capacity. Two quarts better. The only reliable ones are those in which the filtering medium is *thrown away* frequently and replaced by new. Maignen's 'filtre rapide' is excellent. You cannot trust to the best filter to *purify* water. Boil all water, let it stand to deposit sediment, and then filter, solely to improve the taste.
One ewer and basin. One soap-dish.	Granite ware from the Atmospheric Churn Company, 119, New Bond Street, W., is the best. Almost all other enamelled ware chips, and retains the smell permanently if left dirty.
One lantern for kerosene. Spare glasses for kerosene. Spare wick for kerosene.	A real hurricane lantern is good; but many 'hurricane lanterns' go out with a mere puff of wind.
One kerosine oil-tin with screw top—1 quart. Kerosine oil, one 40-lb. tin. One bull's-eye lantern. One oil-tin, screw top, ½ pint. One 4-lb. tin of oil. Spare wick. Four dozen boxes of matches.	Obtainable at Zanzibar. Only used occasionally; but the oil can be bartered if found too much. Soldered up in tins of 1 dozen each is the safest way.
One luminous matchbox-case.	Very useful in tent at night; but must be exposed to light for an hour or two daily.
One tube candlestick. Spare globes for candlestick. Candles for candlestick.	The 'silver torch' is a very good one. A candle can be packed

One sheet of Willesden canvas, 10 ft. by 12 ft., with eyelets and loops.
Tent-pegs and mallet.
Drill, 30 yards.
Small rope, 30 yards.
Hammock-twine, 3 hanks.
Three strong needles for twine.
Six 'Charity' or 'Art' blankets.
Three old blazers or sweaters, or flannel shirts.
Two 'policeman's' capes.

anywhere, and is ready at a moment's notice. Therefore often more useful than an oil-lamp.
For use as luggage-tent in wet weather. Stretched over the hammock-pole, it makes a good shelter for men also.
Divide into three lots for two headmen and two servants to make their own tentes d'abris.

Two for servants. Two for headmen. Two for sick porters.
For sick men with diarrhœa or chest troubles.
For messengers in rainy season.
N.B.—Tents, blankets, etc., must be *lent;* on no account given as presents, or they will be bartered for food or drink the first opportunity.

One net-hammock, largest size.
One Willesden canvas awning, 4 ft. by 2 ft. 3 in., lined with thick green baize, to tie *over* hammock-pole.

The largest size is not too large for even a small man.
Made with light wooden slips along edges and down centre for strength. To take out for packing. This awning should have hanging sides and ends of same material, which can be let down or fastened up according to the position of the sun.

Hammock-pole.

Ten-foot bamboo. Obtained at Zanzibar.

Waterproof blanket, about 6 ft. by 4 ft.

Edgington keeps good ones. Very useful to lay on camp-bed if it happens to get wet. For short journeys from camp it can be taken instead of a bed. For this purpose it should be laid on a thick layer of dried grass. If the bath gets worn out, this blanket placed over

Clothes pegs, ½ gross.	*Very* necessary articles, which are usually forgotten.
Alarum.	Necessary for early marches. No wild animal would enter a tent at night where an alarum was ticking. A luminous face would be very useful. N.B.—All luminous articles shine well at night after exposure to the brilliant African sunshine.
Two tweed suits, *unlined*.	Clothes should be purchased from the traveller's *own* tailor and bootmaker. The outfitter has never seen the traveller before, probably expects never to see him again, and can hardly be expected to take as much interest in him as his regular tradesman will.
Two canvas suits for marching and hunting.	If hunting is the traveller's aim, one more canvas and one less tweed suit would be best.
One or two flannel suits.	After a long march or hunt, the traveller will find it best to have a bath (a scooped-out hollow in the ground can be used to bathe in) and change into flannels.
Flannel shirts with good collar-bands, but *no collars*.	
Three travelling (or other caps.	For use at night and in hammock. A 'Tam-o'-Shanter' with a padded crown is useful for wearing in camp.
Two helmets.	Both cheap and good in Zanzibar.
Cotton and woollen socks.	Woollen for marching. Cotton for camp.
Brown-leather, broad-toed, thick-soled boots.	For marching. *Thick* soles to prevent the hot soil from blistering the feet.
Spare laces.	A pair of spare soles, with the necessary nails useful for repairing boots.
Strong, thick-soled slippers.	For use in camp.

Comfortable, easy slippers.	For evenings, and during convalescence.
One pair of lasts for boots.	Wooden lasts in sections, with an iron sole screwed on. The iron sole is for use when boots are to be mended.
Two pair thin cork soles.	The lasts should always be put into boots when they are damp, and cork soles under them for fear of iron-mould.
Light, large, woollen shawl.	To protect the back when marching away from the sun; to be worn as a cummerbund when marching towards it.
Waterproof overcoat, hood, and leggings.	Not mackintosh. The leggings are very useful for walking through grass soaked by the early morning dew.
Light, warm overcoat.	For evenings and night-watches.
Linen towels.	
Turkish towels.	
Six Pyjama suits.	
Two strong, white or coloured, umbrellas.	The black umbrella with a white cover is too heavy to be carried in comfort. The best sort is a white or coloured umbrella, with a second *inside* lining like a parasol has. The inside lining being small might be thick, without much increasing the weight.
Camphor, solid and powdered.	Keep plenty amongst clothes, on account of insects.
One copper kettle.	
One small flat block-tin kettle.	For quick boiling.
Four seamless steel saucepans—nested.	Seamless steel is the best material. The native servants can keep them clean with sand, which would soon wear a hole through a tin saucepan. Iron saucepans break; copper ones want re-tinning.
Two large sufurias.	For baking and roasting. Obtained at Zanzibar. Large

Cooking Appliances

One small sufuria.

One seamless steel fry-pan.
One circular fry-pan with handle bent up at right angles to pan, and bent again at right angles to that; so that the final arm lies 5 inches above and horizontal to pan.
Three round tins for baking bread—nested.
One hot-water plate and cover.

Two saucepan brushes.
Two dishes, granite ware, deep.
One pudding-dish, granite ware.
Two jugs, 1 quart each, granite ware.
One meat-saw.

One chopper.
One mincing-machine.

Two wire sieves.
Two muslin safes

One kitchen fork.
Two iron spoons.
Four dozen dusters.

Small spirit-stove.

enough to hold fry-pan mentioned below.
For native servants. The only way to prevent the master's sufuria being used.

With this apparatus a joint or loaf of bread can be lowered into and taken out of a hot sufuria, without running the risk of dropping it into the ashes or dirt.
One for use. Two stored away.
A great convenience. It is very difficult to serve anything up hot with a high wind blowing.

Meat will not keep unless it is cleanly and neatly cut into joints.

Very useful. Most meat is tough. But tough meat minced and cooked with herbs and condiments is very palatable.
For flour, in making bread.
The cylindrical safes sold everywhere. But they must be re-covered with *very fine* muslin.

One dozen each to be marked with red or blue square or circle. Each servant will then know his own duster, and which duster for which use.
Very useful in rain when no

Methylated spirit.	hut is near, or at night during illness.
	Four 1-pint tins corked, and tin-caps *well* soldered over neck.
Four *rivetted* buckets.	Two sizes, to nest in pairs. One painted blue for washing up crockery in. Natives may borrow this one only to fetch their water-supply in.
Six meat hooks.	
One cross-cut saw.	
One rip-saw.	
One saw-file.	
Two files.	
One large screwdriver.	
One small screwdriver.	
One pair pincers.	
One pair pliers (and wire-cutter).	
One screw-wrench.	
One strong heavy hammer.	
One stone chisel.	Very useful for cutting open packing-cases.
One small axe.	
One spring balance to weigh 100 lb.	
Four strong padlocks.	Keys to be tied on.
Four hasps. } Four pair hinges. }	{ Screws to fit to be packed with them.
One sailor's palm.	
Carpet and packing-needles.	
Strong thread and wax.	
One pair strong scissors for general use.	
One pair long scissors for cutting hair.	
One pair lamp-scissors.	Natives cut wicks badly with ordinary scissors.
Two strong knives with swivels.	
Three gimlets.	
Three bradawls.	
Two trowels.	For digging holes for poles, for rough tents, etc. If the traveller intends to build a

Scientific Instruments 329

Screws, nails, tintacks.	
One native hoe.	temporary house, it is well to take a 4-inch Archimedian screwdrill.
	Buy in Zanzibar. For clearing ground for tent.
Six native axes.	For cutting timber for temporary house.
Two native billhooks.	For cutting timber for temporary house, and for cutting firewood.
One dozen long butchers' knives.	For cutting grass for thatching.
Collars and chains.	If dogs are taken.
Aneroid.	
Telescope.	
Thermometer.	
Pocket compass.	With half face luminous.
Tape-measure.	Thirty feet or more.
Drawing instruments and appliances.	
Book, 'Hints to Travellers,' Royal Geographical Society.	Also any instruments in this which the traveller knows how to use. The Royal Geographical Society teach intending travellers the use of instruments.
Writing-case.	Well fitted. A writing-board or 'knee-table' is useful.
Almanack.	
Diary.	
Letter-weigher.	
Extra ink.	Pack with oil for lamps.
Strong waterproof envelopes.	For sending mails to coast.
American cloth, 6 yards.	For wrapping mails and parcels in for transport to coast.
Toilet paper.	
Two whistles.	Two notes. One for calling headman. One for servant.
Small label for each key.	
Straps—2 large, 2 small.	Pack away, or natives will borrow to use as belts.
Large rat-traps.	For small animals. Other traps if desired.

Appendix

Hydrochlorate of strychnine, 4 oz.	For troublesome carnivora.
Four small cheap cartridge bags.	For headmen.
Two small cheap revolvers and ammunition, with cases and belts.	For messengers. No one will attack a messenger with a revolver: and a native with a revolver never hits what he aims at. Revolvers ensure safety without bloodshed.
Fine strong rope, 3 doz. yards.	
Thick twine.	
Fine string.	
Wash leather.	For polishing instruments, etc.
Sapolio or Monkey Brand soap.	For cleaning metal.
'Huswif.'	Containing: needles, pins, safety-pins, buttons, thread, cotton, tape and plenty of webbing, etc.
Paper fasteners.	Loose papers are a great trouble on a journey.
India-rubber bands.	
Gum.	One bottle. Glue is useless in the tropics.
Hand-mirrors.	A few useful for barter, and in case mirror in dressing-case breaks.
Bucket with seat.	Painted red. This will prevent its being used for other purposes.
Bed-pan.	Pack the above three articles in one load with lamps and oil.
Chamber, granite ware.	
Reeded air-cushion, 28 in. by 18 in.	In fevers makes a soft mattress for body. But needs two blankets at least over it for comfort and ventilation.
India-rubber water-bottle.	With hot water to feet or stomach in dysentery. With cold water as a pillow in fever.
Two invalid cups.	
Night-light shade.	

The Luncheon Basket 331

One pair of blue-glass spectacles, wire-gauze sides.

Guns and ammunition for men.

Barter articles for journey.

Necessary after fever, when the eyes cannot bear the glare of the sun.

Best obtained in Zanzibar.

Mr. Muxworthy of Messrs. Bonstead, Ridley and Co., Zanzibar, obtained everything of this sort for me. I owe him many a debt of gratitude for his never-failing kindness and courtesy, and for much valuable advice.

Medicine chest.

Will be described in separate pamphlet. See Preface.

'Luncheon-basket.' Containing:
One box of matches.
One teapot, granite ware.
One strainer to hang on spout.
One tea-cosy (small).
One small coffee-pot.
One milk-jug, granite ware.
One slop-basin, granite ware.
One china-basin (for soup).
One china-mug.
Two china-plates.
Two granite-ware egg-cups.
Two small tumblers in wickerwork.

Made of strong basketwork, covered outside with waterproof material. One half divided in compartments up to top of basket; the other half divided halfway up, and the upper portion of this half filled by a tray similarly divided. The lid with straps and bands to hold knives, forks, spoons and plates.

One wickerwork-covered bottle for salt.
One wickerwork-covered bottle for mustard.
One pepper castor with solid and perforated caps.
Game carving-knife and fork.
Two large knives.
Two small knives.
One steel for sharpening.
Two large forks.

All bottles should fit easily, but not too loosely into their compartments.

All knives with 'lockfast' handles.

Any enamelled ware is inconveniently light and unstable for general use; and enamelled cups and basins are very unin-

Two small forks.
Two table-spoons.
Two dessert-spoons.
Four tea-spoons.
Two egg-spoons.
One salt-spoon.

One corkscrew.
Three dusters.
Two wickerwork-covered bottles for fluids.
One wickerwork-covered bottle, wide-mouthed, for butter.
One wickerwork-covered bottle, for condensed milk.
One wickerwork-covered bottle, for jam or marmalade.
One granite-ware bottle for sugar.
One small tin canister for tea.
One metal or eathenware case for bread or biscuits.
Two or three small canisters for extra goods.
One cardboard box with four divisions to hold four eggs.
One sardine opener.
Spare corks.

viting for a sick or tired man to drink from. It is best, therefore, to have china-mugs and plates, and granite ware only to fall back upon when these are broken.

Pack elsewhere one or two spare china-mugs, basins and plates, two or three glasses to fit wickerwork cases, one or two bottles, and a granite ware mug, and two plates.

If room can be found, a flat, one-pint kettle would be handy kept in the luncheon-basket. The porter who carries luncheon-basket must be a quick man, and have no other load; this will enable him to arrive in camp as soon as, or before his master.

The top must fasten on securely.

The traveller should take a small cookery-book with him, and learn how to cook a few useful dishes himself. Especially let him learn as many ways as he can of cooking eggs, an article of food always plentiful in Africa. The native servant will always test the eggs first in a basin of water to see if they lie quietly at the bottom, and in this way the traveller can *usually depend on being well supplied with fairly good eggs.*

STORES FOR DAILY USE.

Boxes of wood or strong wickerwork, containing the following stores for daily use :
 Sauce, own bottle.
 Custard-powder, own tin.
 Brandy, own flask.
 Potted meat, own tin.
 Marmalade, own tin.
 Jam, own tin.
 Liebig, own pot.
 Mixed herbs, own bottle.
 Soap (4 lb.), light wooden box.
 Soup (2 tins), own tin.
 Sugar (moist, 4 lb.), granite bottle.
 Sugar (castor, 1 lb.), granite bottle.
 Raspberry vinegar, own bottle.

 Montserrat lime-juice, own bottle.

 American beef marrow (Libby's), glass bottle.
 Tapioca, granite bottle.
 Bacon, own tin.

 Butter (Danish, 2 tins), own tins.

Boxes 34 in. by 13 in. by 10 in. inside measurement will hold one load of supplies. If made of wood, the boxes should fasten by a hasp and padlock; but the hasp-fittings must be continued as an iron or brass band half round box to prevent their being torn off. The padlocks should fasten with a spring, only requiring a key to open them. The bottom of the wooden boxes, and for an inch or two up the side, should be covered with tin or *light* copper sheeting, on account of the danger of white ants. Basket-work boxes should be covered with strong waterproofing, which white ants rarely touch. Really strong baskets are better but more expensive than boxes.

Lime-juice and raspberry-vinegar will disguise the taste of dirty and almost undrinkable water.

Open bacon-tin, and warm in front of fire; then pour loose melted fat into a bottle, and replace the bacon in its own tin. It will not now leak and damage the other stores. Bacon is useful for occasional use to replace butter. African meat has no fat, which an Englishman needs *in moderation* even in the tropics.

All glass bottles should be sewn up in corrugated paper,

Biscuits (8 lb.), in own tins.
Chocolat Menier (½ lb.), granite bottle.
Coffee (½ lb.), tin bottle.
Tea (½ lb.), granite bottle.
Curry-powder, own bottle.
Essence of lemon, own bottle.
Arrowroot (½ lb.), tin bottle.
Baking - powder (Dakin's), own bottle.
Knife-powder, 1 small tin.
Rangoon oil, screw-cap tin.
Condensed milk (2 tins), own tins.
Oatmeal (2 lb.), granite bottle.
Symington's pea-flour (½ lb.), tin bottle.
White pepper (1 lb.), tin bottle.
Salt (2 lb.), granite bottle.
Mustard, own small bottle.
Cardboard egg-box, with divisions for two dozen eggs. Inside light wooden box.

leaving the mouth alone exposed, and have screw-caps or solid india-rubber corks. Any chemist will supply them.

Woolf and Co., 119, New Bond Street, W., supply glass, tin, and granite-ware bottles. The tin bottles should have corks, strengthened by discs of tin above and below. Their wide - mouth, screw - capped glass bottles should be sewn up in corrugated paper, with only the mouth exposed.

The supplies necessary for the daily-store boxes should be taken out to Africa in their own tins, etc., packed in an ordinary packing-case ; and the special bottles which have been taken out empty filled just before the march begins.

RESERVE STORES.

In cases weighing 60 lb. to 62 lb. when packed. Any shape.

Biscuits (plain), 90 lb.
Biscuits (sweet), 6 lb.
Chocolat Menier, or chocolate and milk, or cocoa, or cocoa and milk, or all four, 12 lb.

Arrowroot, 6 lb.

Baking - powder (Dakin's), 12 bottle.

The lids should be screwed on only, so that they can be easily opened and reclosed.

As far as possible a small quantity of everything should be in each box, so that it need not be necessary to open many cases at once. Each article should be in its own soldered-up tin, so that the cases need not be tin-lined.

Useful for sick natives, as well as for the traveller.
The cook should know how to bake bread. Any good native cook at the coast can.

Groceries

Australian or other tinned meat, 6 tins.	For use on occasions when no meat can be obtained. Useful during convalescence. Even Australian tinned meat is a luxury after some months of forest meat.
American beef marrow (Libby's), six 2-lb. tins.	Marrow and lard are needed for cooking with. Bread fried in marrow will take the place of butter if that fails.
Lard, twelve 1-lb. tins.	
Coffee (ground and roasted), twelve 1-lb. tins.	Coffee-berries can be purchased at Zanzibar; but they are not cheap, and it is a trouble to roast and grind coffee on a march.
Curry-powder, six half-bottles.	
Essence of lemon, six 2-oz. bottles.	
Corn-flour, 6 lb.	
Knife-powder, 2 tins.	
Milk (sweetened and unsweetened), 24 tins.	Milk can occasionally be obtained on the march; but it is expensive, and does not keep. It is safest to boil it as soon as bought. Unsweetened tinned milk will only keep fresh about thirty-six hours in the tropics.
Night-lights (10-hour), 3 boxes.	
Oatmeal, twelve 2-lb. tins.	More or less according to taste.
Symington's pea-flour, 6 lb.	A prepared pea-flour very useful for making soup quickly.
Pepper (white), 3 lb.	Excess can be bartered.
Salt, 90 lb.	Best packed in paper packets of one or two pounds each. Each dozen pounds soldered up in a separate tin. It is very useful for barter.
Soap (toilet) 24 tablets.	
Soap (bar), 90 lb.	For washing clothes and for barter. Can be wrapped in waterproof paper, and packed in ordinary packing-cases.

Sauce, 12 half-bottles.	African meat often tough and tasteless. Sauce very acceptable.
Soups, 1 dozen tins.	Necessary during convalescence.
Sugar (brown), 70 lb.	For cooking and barter. Should be soldered up in tins of 10 lb. each.
Sugar (castor or lump), 12 lb.	In 2-lb. tins.
Tea, 10 lb.	In 1-lb. tins.
Fruits in syrup, 4 tins.	Useful during convalescence.
Bacon, four 3-lb. tins.	
Butter (Danish), 18 tins.	Open tin. Wash butter well, and put it in glass bottle (in luncheon basket) with some water. Renew the water *daily*.
Jam, marmalade, and potted meats.	According to taste.
Tinned sardines and herrings.	These fish, wrapped in clean writing-paper and fried, are very useful during convalescence.
Liebig, four 2-oz. pots.	For flavouring Symington's pea-flour. Useful during convalescence, or after a long tiring march. It is a very useful stimulant, though not a food.
Edward's dessicated soups.	Very useful if the traveller learns how to use them.
Flour, six 28-lb. tins.	Bought at Zanzibar. Two tins are put up in a light wooden case, and make one load.
Washing soda, 6 lb.	
Oil for guns and instruments.	
Custard powder, 12 tins.	
Brandy, 3 bottles.	
Guns and ammunition.	The traveller can easily decide for himself, or consult some better guide than the author of this book.

PACKING.

Dress wickerwork baskets covered with dull canvas.	Light; very good, but expensive.
Indian or other air-tight cases.	Outside wooden cases unnecessary. Very good for boxes which will need to be often opened; but expensive.
Cabin trunks.	Will not keep clothes quite so dry or free from insects as Indian cases; but keep them well, and two hours of tropical sunshine will dry anything, however damp. They are good, strong, cheap, and useful.
Linen hampers, or strong square baskets.	Need to be covered with waterproofing; good, but expensive.
Small travelling-baths.	Useful; but rather a trouble to undo frequently, on account of the strap. A basket-case is necessary for the outside for protection on the voyage. This basket-case is cheap, and very useful afterwards to carry kitchen-pots in on the march.
Valises.	A great trouble; a valise needs a clean floor to be packed and unpacked upon. This is out of the question on the march. Cabin-trunks answer better.
Wooden boxes.	Described under 'stores for daily use.'
Dirty clothes-bags.	One or two useful for dirty clothes, tent-pegs, etc.
'Willesden' canvas-bags; 3 ft. deep, 2 ft. diameter, with strap and padlock at mouth.	One or two useful for clothes, blankets, etc.; and for fetching rice or grain from a distance.
Portmanteau.	A small one is a decided convenience.
Hand-bag.	For writing-materials, account-book, keys, and other small articles which are wanted for daily use.

As far as possible, all necessary supplies should be scattered through several boxes; so that the loss of one box may never cause the loss of all the cartridges, or salt, or butter, as might otherwise be the case.

A small tin of biscuits in each box of clothes will save the traveller from having to wait for food, in case of any accident or delay to his luncheon basket on the march.

All boxes should be plainly marked *at the ends*, so that the mark may be visible, and the box identified whilst it is being carried by the porter on the march.

An invoice of contents should be fastened inside lid of every box.

There should also be a book with an invoice of the contents of every box and package, and opposite each entry the name of the porter who carries it.

All wickerwork, tin, or leather cases should be packed together in one or two strong packing-cases, for safety on the voyage out.

These lists are made out for one traveller on the supposition that he will be away twelve months, that he will often be able to obtain only meat, fowls, and eggs, and sometimes not even these, and that he will be ill for two months of the time. Two travellers would require very little more than one, and three not much more.

www.ingramcontent.com/pod-product-compliance
Lightning Source LLC
Chambersburg PA
CBHW021817300426
44114CB00009BA/202